I0813618

Sure Thing DESSERTS

Sure Thing DESSERTS

TRULY PERFECT VERSIONS *of* EVERYDAY CLASSICS

MATT LEWIS

ABRAMS, NEW YORK

Editor: Holly Dolce
Designers: Deb Wood and Sarah Gifford
Design Manager: Danielle Youngsmith
Managing Editor: Jodi Wong
Production Manager: Alison Gervais and Larry Pekarek

Library of Congress Control Number: 2025931146

ISBN: 978-1-4197-4932-2
eISBN: 979-8-89684-013-8

Printed and bound in China
10 9 8 7 6 5 4 3 2 1

ABRAMS is represented in the UK and Europe
by Abrams & Chronicle Books, 1 West Smithfield, London EC1A 9JU
and Média-Participations, 57 rue Gaston Tessier, 75166 Paris, France.
abramsandchronicle.co.uk and media-participations.com
info@abramsandchronicle.co.uk

CONTENTS

BARS AND BROWNIES (AND A CRISP)

COOKIES

CAKES: SHEET, STACKED, AND LOAF STYLE

MORNING STUFF

INTRODUCTION
STILL BAKING / *Less* FUSSY

MY LIFE IN CAKE

If you view my biography from a bird's-eye vantage point, it is blatantly obvious that baking or baked goods have always been part of my DNA. My baking fascination started early, and it continues to this day. But my life in cakes and cookies and brownies and bread was never predestined; it was always floating in the periphery—a bit circuitous and spotty, and in retrospect, it was always the surest thing about me.

Growing up, my mom was always happy to bend the rules of the food pyramid so that we could occasionally share cake for breakfast or bonbons for dinner, as long as I promised to keep our irregular diet a secret between us. Looking back, the quality of our baked goods at this time was questionable. We were not eating Parisian-level pastry. This was Florida in the 1980s. It was strip malls and franchises and quick-serve concepts; sadly, I can't remember crossing the door of a mom-and-pop cafe or bakery or restaurant during this time. We subsisted on boxed cake mixes, industrial-style grocery store cookies, and fast-food soft-serve. But frankly, I simply didn't care. I didn't know better yet. I was both happy to have whatever baked goods were available and to share a secret with my mom.

In college, I continued my alarming input of all things sweet. I ate my fair share of overly manufactured muffins wrapped in plastic and sad croissants that had the texture of supermarket white bread, but on occasion I was able to sample new things just outside the campus perimeter. I was studying in the Deep South and, if I looked hard enough, I would stumble upon restaurants that served things like homemade pecan pie, big bouffant-style cakes, and jars of pudding. But these treats were the exceptions. I was a fairly broke student and didn't look too far beyond the university cafeteria. If there were bakeries farther outside the college campus, I was unaware of them.

Post-college, I moved to New York City, which accelerated and intensified my dessert curiosity. There are many reasons for this, but there are two primary ones. First, I was well within commuting distance of my grandmother for the first time in my life. She was an excellent cook and a fabulous baker and always made a glorious over-the-top cheesecake for me each and every time I visited. She made other sweets for me as well, but it was her towering, tangy, lemon cheesecake—so rich and creamy, each bite felt like a small luxury—that changed my dessert worldview. Second, well, I was living in a world-class city. For me, at that time, it was *the* world-class city. New York was a revelation, an embarrassment of riches. It offered an overwhelming, staggering number of options and flavors, and the fresh (and not always so fresh) pastries reflected distinct and overlapping cultures. It was still many, many years before the bakery renaissance would take hold. This was before Magnolia Bakery burst on the scene, and you would have been hard-pressed to find a swoon-worthy baguette, but I could still walk down most any block and spot something—whatever the quality—that I wanted to try for dessert.

During my first few years in the city, I floated between a few long-term jobs in the entertainment and advertising worlds while taking sporadic chocolate and baking classes at night. The classes were not intense—they were more of the continuing education ilk—but I was learning the fundamentals and beyond, and a few of the instructors were downright inspiring. More importantly, the classes only made the gravitational pull of baking stronger.

Then, a few things happened in quick succession that would throw me fully into the dessert sphere. My baking hobby suddenly became an all-encompassing career. I spent the next fourteen years in the small business world of chocolate and baking. It seems a bit absurd to try and pack this part of my life into a few small paragraphs, but I am also aware that this is an intro to a book and not my autobiography or memoir.

In the early 2000s, I decided I wanted to open a boutique chocolate store that would sell the most beautiful collection of confections and bars from a curated selection of famous chocolatiers. Weirdly, this retail format didn't really exist yet. Even more bizarre to reflect on, retail rents were laughably manageable, almost fairy tale–like by today's standards. This made it entirely feasible to open a store on a shoestring. After just a few months of prepping, with no real-world experience, I opened Chocolate Bar with a business partner, Alison McGonigal.

I suppose you could say it was successful. Alison and I worked extremely hard every single day. We had several regular customers, and we sold fantastic chocolate, but we lacked sleep and retail experience. We even published a cookbook together named after our establishment. After the book came out, I decided I wanted to pursue the making of baked goods (brownies, cookies, cakes) instead of just selling other people's chocolate confections. Alison was initially on board, and we took on a new founder, Renato Poliafito, to open a bakery in a less-expensive neighborhood. Manhattan was starting to become increasingly less fairy tale–like in the rent department, and Brooklyn was still somewhat affordable.

Things changed. Alison and I were not always aligned. I left Chocolate Bar, Alison remained as sole owner, and Renato and I pursued the bakery venture on our own.

Baked, our small bakery in Red Hook, Brooklyn, opened in 2005. It was not an easy opening. We had many construction setbacks and financial setbacks and, perhaps even more problematically, neither Renato nor I had any restaurant or food-service training. Thankfully, we had youth and naiveté on our side.

We also had a bit of luck. Two icons, Martha Stewart and Oprah Winfrey, gave our bakery major press shout-outs shortly after opening. We needed it. It basically changed our business from a sleepy bakery to a brownie powerhouse. A lot of other stuff happened during our time running this bakery. We co-wrote four cookbooks (two of which sold extremely well). We opened branches in Charleston, Manhattan, and Tokyo. We launched a line of specialty glass bakeware with one of the oldest glass manufacturers in the United States, and we created several fancy boxed baking mixes for the likes of Williams Sonoma, Sur La Table, and Whole Foods.

It wasn't all rainbows. We battled stress and drama and fatigue on the daily. It was like being immersed in baking school and business school while also attempting to juggle a semblance of a personal life. It was tough but rewarding. I only wish I had a diary of all the baked goods I ate during this stretch. I am sure an outsider looking in would be alarmed by the forkfuls of cake I ate (testing, I was always testing) or the cookies and whoopie pies I consumed in lieu of lunch, or the brownies I brought home as "treats." Often, someone would say something along the lines of "I bet you are sick of cookies (or muffins or loaves or cake)." And somewhat surprisingly, I wasn't. I was ready for a change, though.

Renato and I exited Baked near the beginning of the COVID-19 pandemic. We were planning our exit prior, and the pandemic just hastened things. It was a great bakery, brought to life by great employees, but we both felt it was time for new chapters.

HOW I BAKE NOW

Escape! Everyone was looking for some sort of escape during the pandemic: beaches, mountains, the Great Plains. The city was emptying out. My partner and I had already started to build what was supposed to be our "country" house pre-pandemic, but it quickly became apparent that this would become our only and primary residence. In short order, we let our Brooklyn residential lease lapse, moved into a temporary set-up with family in Woodstock, New York, during the construction of our upstate house, and set about finding our pandemic footing.

We formed a tight-knit COVID-pod with friends and family, and we watched a lot of TV and played a lot of board games together. We also cooked and grilled a lot. Occasionally, over video, I would try to troubleshoot sourdough starter issues for my friends, because everyone was making sourdough bread. During the days,

I busied myself with a few side gigs before landing a really fulfilling full-time job in the tech industry. At night, after everyone fell asleep, I would attempt to read books, cookbooks, and the *New York Times*.

This is the period that cemented my current baking style. I was never an overly fussy baker, but I became even less so. I still enjoyed baking immensely, but I started to condense my old recipes into fewer steps to save time and to eliminate bowls that had to be washed. First, I stopped sifting dry ingredients. It was drilled into me since my very first baking class that you should sift dry ingredients (and, yes, I am aware of why), but I just got over sifting ingredients together when a quick whisking would work equally well in 99.9 percent of all recipes.

Other things I stopped doing that have yet to affect any final product: I stopped measuring vanilla extract and started to go with my gut and eyeball it. I stopped rotating pans halfway through the bake time, since my oven was mostly calibrated. I stopped making things that required a lot of ingredients. I kept simplifying. I only made recipes that had been converted to weights and almost never used my cup measures. I fell madly in love with sheet cakes due to their ease (I was never a fantastic cake decorator) and rarely made three-layer cakes unless it was a super special occasion. Essentially, I found a baking style that worked for my new life: a less structured, upstate life that was not centered professionally around baking.

I still bake a lot. I still eat vast amounts of sweets, and I still love to entertain. But, while I may always have homemade refrigerated cookie dough ready to deploy for guests and late-night treats, the cookie dough is from a recipe that took twenty minutes to pull together and not one of those three-day affairs.

WHAT IS A *Sure Thing* DESSERT?

The desserts in this book are my Sure Things.

Sure Thing desserts are people pleasers. They are guaranteed to please a wide audience. After much time in the professional baking world, I am well aware that chocolate, caramel, peanut butter, and vanilla desserts are almost always preferred over new or trendy ingredients. Sure Thing desserts are mostly easy to make. Most of the recipes in this book are fairly easy to pull together. While the range of skill needed throughout leans toward the beginner with a few just shy of moderate, no recipe is overly complicated. Also, sure thing recipes are more reflective of the average family's needs. No more recipes for a 9 by 13-inch pan of brownies or a yield of fifty cookies.

Sure Thing desserts reflect me. The desserts at Baked were a shared vision between myself and Renato and the entire baking staff, but this book is purely a consideration of my baking style.

This collection of recipes is my greatest hits of sorts. A few of these recipes predate my days at Baked, like a richer version of Nick Malgieri's grand-maman's cake (see page 56), and a portion of these recipes are reworked Baked classics (I had to include an ode to the Baked brownie on page 46), newly minted to complement my current lifestyle. I also included a few recipes that started elsewhere before bending them slightly to my will, such as Tara O'Brady's insanely easy chocolate chip cookie (page 44). Perhaps my favorite recipes are the ones that I tasked my recipe developers to create. These are recipes where I found an impeccable dessert in the wild, like the cornbread blondie (see page 73) at Inness (a resort in upstate New York), and had Cynthia Jordan recreate it for me. Mind you, Cynthia never once tasted this cornbread blondie, she just had me describe it in detail before she went into full-kitchen-magic mode and made a version that was decidedly different but equally delicious. It is now in my heavy recipe rotation. As is the homage to the chocolate rye buttermilk loaf I consumed at Lannan Bakery in Edinburgh, Scotland. Alex Roberts, a true baking wizard, was able to create something that was unique and tasty (and chocolaty) based purely off a photo. The loaf cake (see page 159), one of my favorite things in a book full of favorite things, is not a replica of the cake I had in Edinburgh, but it is Alex's view of what this cake could be.

This cookbook is more than just recipes to me. It is a diary of memories and moments marked in cakes and cookies. I do not expect anyone to become as attached to these recipes as I am, but I hope they bring a lot of happiness to your future gatherings. Of course, I hope a few of them become your regular staples in frequent rotation. I encourage you to riff off them and make them your own. Above all else, enjoy and have fun. I was always a bit leery of the common "baking is a science" refrain, as it drains the color from baking into a gray, dull, lab-like task. Baking can be specific, but it is also artistic and personal and fanciful and forgiving.

Be free and bake.

Sincerely,
Matt

THE SIMPLIFIED BAKER'S TOOL KIT

(EQUIPMENT, TOOLS, AND INGREDIENTS)

Simplify! Pare down! These are my new-ish baking mantras. It's not always easy because I covet newfangled pans and tools and exotic ingredients. But, overall, I have been able to consolidate my kitchen wares into a tight, nimble assortment.

All of the recipes in this book can be made with this leaner list of equipment, tools, and ingredients. Also, I did my best to note, via asterisk, items that are "nice to have" but aren't absolutely necessary for Sure Thing baking.

APPLIANCES

Stand Mixer

Stand mixers are a bit of a splurge, but they are a game changer. If you like to bake or cook with any frequency, they are a must-have. I have been using the Kitchen-Aid brand stand mixers for as long as I can remember, and they tend to last forever. In fact, my first Kitchen Aid mixer lasted for fourteen years and would have lasted longer if I didn't accidentally drop it. Regardless of the brand, make sure you get something sturdy, with all the attachments.

*Microwave**

I don't currently own a microwave. I sometimes think about getting one again if only to melt butter and chocolate, but that feels like an extravagance. If you do own one, it is my preferred melting method (less mess, faster). If you don't own one, no worries, you can easily melt chocolate using the double-boiler method on page 33.

KITCHEN EQUIPMENT

Cooling Rack(s)

Truthfully, you only need one (possibly two) really sturdy, cooling rack/sheet. Look for something in stainless steel so you can push it through the dishwasher without any rusting issues. At one point, I had stacks of cooling racks, but it turns out that unless you are running a bakery out of your house, this is really unnecessary.

Ice-Cream Scoop

Get an ice-cream scoop with a release mechanism. I have a few sizes, and, oddly, I don't use any of them to scoop ice cream since they are not built to withstand super frozen pints. Instead, I use mine to portion cake and cupcake batter and scoop the perfect cookie dough balls.

Measuring Cups

Dry.* I grew up in an age where nearly all American cookbooks were written in cups and imperial measurements, and I became quite comfortable working in this realm. But . . . trust me, break this habit. Your baking will be faster and your ingredient measurements will be more accurate with a kitchen scale (my favorite kitchen tool). However, if you don't have a scale, there is nothing wrong with using the tried-and-true dry measuring cups. They often come in a set of four: ¼ cup, ⅓ cup, ½ cup, 1 cup. Look for a sturdy set that can be tossed in the dishwasher.

Liquid. This is simple. Look for a heavy glass 2-cup liquid measuring cup with demarcations that won't wash off. They are perfect for measuring liquids, and you can pop it in the microwave to melt butter and chocolate.

Measuring Spoons

It is quite possible I have had my measuring spoon set for twenty-plus years. I prefer the heavy-duty metal variety, held together with a ring so they are less likely to go missing.

Microplane

Microplane is actually a preferred brand of grater, long and thin. It is incredibly handy for zesting lemons and other citrus. Of course, mine also does double-duty as a means of grating a small hunk of Parmesan over plated pasta. Obviously, it works wonders on other hard cheeses as well. And spices! Don't forget spices. My current Microplane has been washed well over a thousand times and it looks the same as it did on the day I bought it.

Mixing Bowls

I recommend a simple set of nested metal or glass mixing bowls. They are easy to clean, easy to store, and usually lightweight. However, I know the pull of a decorative vintage ceramic mixing bowl, especially a beautiful bowl that can double as tableware. Or maybe you were drawn to a plastic (really lightweight and manageable) set with a pour spout. In the end, it doesn't really matter which mixing bowl you use, as long as it is food safe and dishwasher safe (well, this detail means a great deal to me because I try to avoid hand washing at all costs).

Parchment Paper

If you bake, you need parchment paper. Parchment paper is used as a pan liner for your cookies, cakes, loaves, and bars. It prevents your baked goods from sticking and it makes cleaning up a bit easier. In my opinion, you should buy the least expensive option available. I don't really have a favorite brand, as they all seem to work equally well. Oh, and when baking cookies, I tend to get multiple uses out of my parchment, which feels both economical and greener.

*Pastry Cutter**

A pastry cutter (a.k.a. pastry blender) is an inexpensive handheld tool made up of several wires in a horseshoe shape connected to a wooden or steel handle. The tool is extremely helpful for cutting cold butter or shortening into flour for biscuits, scones, pie doughs, and other pastry. Do you need a pastry cutter? Not really. You can achieve the same cutting technique with the tines of a fork or, in some cases, a quick pulse through a food processor, but I value my pastry cutter for its simplicity.

Kitchen Scale

If you bake, even semi-frequently, I implore you to buy a digital kitchen scale. A kitchen scale accomplishes two things quite effectively. First, it guarantees consistency. Whereas measuring dry ingredients via cup measures is often inconsistent based on several factors (such as whether the ingredient is scooped into a cup versus spooned into a cup), weighing ingredients via a scale ensures dependability each and every time you bake. Second, a digital scale adds efficiency. It is much faster, cleaner, and easier to bake with a scale. For instance, you simply place your mixing bowl on a scale and weigh out the requested amount of flour or sugar or any other dry ingredient directly from your stored ingredients. When using cup measures, you have to spoon the dry ingredients into a cup, level it off, and then add it to the bowl. This adds two more steps and one more item to clean. If you do not want to invest in a scale, fear not, this book is written in both cups and weights.

Spatulas

Rubber. I use three basic rubber spatulas of varying size (small, medium, large) for scraping down bowls, folding egg whites into bowls of batter, and light hand-mixing. Just make sure you invest in a rubber spatula set that is heat-resistant to 500°F (260°C) so it can cut through just-off-the-stove caramel and won't melt on the heat cycle in the dishwasher.

Metal. One of my most-used kitchen tools is my medium-size offset metal spatula, which I use to smooth batters in pans, frost and fill, marble and swirl, and loosen bars and brownies from the sides of their pans after cooling. I highly recommend at least one small or medium offset metal spatula and one regular medium or large flat metal spatula for your baking tool kit.

Whisks

No matter how often or infrequently you bake, you will still want to invest in some sturdy, stainless steel whisks. They should look and feel like they came out of a restaurant supply store, with a nice heft in your hand. I recommend a smaller whisk for blending ingredients in liquid measuring cups, and a medium and large whisk for all of your other whisking needs. Whisks are necessary and great for blending dry ingredients, whipping air into batters, and combining melted butter and chocolate.

Pans and Bakeware

When I set out to write this book, I tried to keep the various pan-size needs to a minimum. As I am a collector of all manner of pans, it was not easy, but I did pare the list back to the casual baker's necessities.

I bake exclusively in light metal pans no matter the dessert, for even bakes and firm, but not crispy, sides. I tend to favor the same types of brands and pans you can find inexpensively on the internet at your local cookware shop. I highly recommend the lightweight aluminum bakeware line by Nordic Ware. Their bakeware range is utilitarian, inexpensive, and easy to clean.

The following pans are used throughout this cookbook:

9-inch (23-cm) round cake pan
8-inch (20-cm) square pan (for cakes, brownies, and bars)
9 by 13-inch (23 by 33-cm) pan (for sheet cakes)
12-cup standard cupcake and muffin tin
9 by 5 by 3-inch (23 by 13 by 7.5-cm) loaf pan
10 to 12-cup (2.4 to 2.8-L) Bundt pan (any shape)
10 inch cast-iron skillet (I use an inexpensive version from Lodge)

Nice to Have, but Not Necessary Pans

9-inch springform pan
10 by 15-inch (25 by 38-cm) jelly roll pan

INGREDIENTS

I no longer own a bakery that I can raid for expensive or hard-to-find ingredients. All of the ingredients used throughout this book are fairly straightforward and should be super easy to find at most grocery stores. I noted some of my favorite brands and things I look for in this section but did not call out every single ingredient used throughout. I am generally agnostic to brands of sugar and flour.

Black Cocoa Powder

I use black cocoa powder in a few recipes in this book, but if you bake often, it is a worthwhile ingredient to have on hand. I love the way it can turn typical cocoa-based cakes and brownies into an ethereal, inky, spooky black color. It offers a lot of visual drama. However, it lacks some of the chocolaty flavor of typical cocoa, so you only want to substitute it for half of the regular cocoa powder if you are adjusting and experimenting with recipes written for traditional cocoa powder. If a recipe calls for ½ cup of cocoa powder, I would use ¼ cup of black cocoa powder and ¼ cup of Dutch-process cocoa powder. This ingredient is not available everywhere, but you can purchase it from KingArthurBaking.com.

Black Sesame Paste (also known as Black Tahini) *

It is highly likely you do not have black sesame paste in your pantry, but it really is a magical ingredient you should seek out online or at your local Asian grocer. Black sesame paste is essentially a thick-ish, glossy paste made from ground toasted black sesame seeds. The flavor profile is rich and nutty. While I use it in only one recipe in this book, Black Sesame White Chocolate Cookies (page 113), I encourage you to find ways to add it to your baked goods. Quick suggestion: Try subbing it one for one in baking recipes that ask for peanut butter.

Butter

I used unsalted butter to test every recipe in this book, but it is totally fine to use salted butter in its place. Perhaps you might opt to decrease the salt in the recipe if you do swap salted for unsalted, but it isn't necessary.

Chocolate

The big, vast world of chocolate is both overwhelming and fascinating. However, for this book, I am only focusing on the fundamentals you need to know to make all the recipes within.

For chocolate chunks: A good-quality chunk is essential for producing a best-in-class cookie. I currently love Guittard chocolate chunks (in milk and dark) that sit alongside some more traditional brands on the grocery shelf. The chunks are variable and organic, and they have a welcome chocolate pop. Note: I only use these bags of chunks or chips as cookie inclusions and not for other applications. If you are feeling more ambitious and a bit spendy, you could invest in a bag of Valrhona's Guanaja chocolate fèves (discs) and chop them up into bite-size chunks yourself.

For icings, ganaches, frostings, and decorations in this book: I recommend about 70 percent cacao for dark chocolate and at least 30 percent cacao for milk chocolate. Look for brands that have a clean ingredient deck. A premium chocolate should only include cocoa butter, cacao, sugar, milk solids, vanilla (potentially), and often a natural emulsifier like soy lecithin. Again, I am a fan of Valrhona's Guanaja (dark) and Jivara (milk) lines, but I have found that the baking bars offered by Ghiradelli are equally pleasing, in addition to being affordable and widely distributed.

Cocoa Powder

I am a huge fan of Valrhona's unsweetened Dutch-process cocoa powder and have used it for many years. Their cocoa is a dark reddish brown, and it adds a smooth chocolaty warmth without tilting into bitter. However, it is not inexpensive. When it goes on sale online or at a specialty retailer, I buy up a bunch of tins. If you are looking for a less expensive alternative, the options are limitless. I don't really have a favorite; I just tend to use what is available to me at the time. I have used Hershey's and private-label store brands in many recipe tests, and I was never displeased with the result.

Rye Flour

There are three amazing recipes (Chocolate Rye Cookies on page 104, Chocolate Malted Rye Loaf Cake with Ganache on page 159, and the Cast-Iron Orange Olive Oil Pancake on page 185) in this book that utilize rye flour. I am aware it is not yet a standard cupboard item, but I tend to always have a bag in my house for bread baking. Rye flour is more earthy and complex (that is, the taste is robust, and you will notice it) than your regular all-purpose flour, but that is why it balances well with many chocolate desserts. Rye flour does not have as much gluten as regular flour, so it cannot be subbed one for one across all of your baking needs. If you want to explore baking with rye in other desserts, I suggest starting with substituting no more than 25 percent to start. (If a recipe calls for 1 cup of all-purpose flour, use ¼ cup of rye and ¾ cup of all-purpose instead.)

Vanilla Extract and Vanilla Paste

Vanilla is expensive, but it keeps forever. If you are going to do a lot of baking, I suggest buying a large bottle. My go-to brand has always been Nielsen-Massey—with its potent and rich vanilla notes—but any pure vanilla extract will do. Vanilla bean paste is thick and fragrant and and made with real vanilla bean seeds. It is ever so slightly more concentrated than extract, but it can be substituted for pure vanilla extract in a one-to-one ratio. I tend to use vanilla bean paste in light-colored frostings and fillings to add a delightful, speckled appearance.

HELPFUL HINTS: HOW TO PREPARE A BUNDT PAN FOR A *Quick and Clean* RELEASE

Bundt cakes are beautiful! They come in many decorative shapes and styles and sizes that easily elevate any party without a lot of fuss.

However, due to the intricate details etched into the Bundt pans, it is essential that you prepare the pan accordingly: Get in there and grease it good, so the Bundt cake releases without bits and pieces sticking to the bottom and sides.

Here are a few proven methods for prepping a Bundt pan:

BUTTER AND FLOUR OR BUTTER AND COCOA POWDER:

This is similar to preparing other cake pans in that you smear room-temperature butter into every surface and crevice of the pan so that it is glistening. There is no need to apply a light touch here. You need this cake to release. Once buttered, sprinkle a few tablespoons of flour (for white/yellow cakes) or a mix of flour/cocoa powder (for chocolate-based cakes) into the bottom of the pan, then turn, rotate, and pat the pan so that the flour or cocoa powder covers every inch (including the tube or well) of the pan. A well-prepared pan should have a heavy flour or cocoa coating before you add the batter.

BAKER'S JOY NONSTICK BAKING SPRAY

I have many baker friends (including the food stylist for this book) who swear by Baker's Joy. It is a flour-based spray that goes on quickly and easily. Again, I err on the heavy-handed side here: There is no harm in giving the pan a second blast of nonstick spray. Make sure it coats every detail of the pan.

HOMEMADE PAN RELEASE A.K.A. CAKE GOOP

I was unaware of the homemade pan release recipe (see below) until it started popping up all over my social feeds a few years back. It is easy, reliable, and well . . . homemade. As always, the goal is to thoroughly cover the pan in the goo.

1 cup (125 g) all-purpose flour
1 cup (120 ml) neutral oil (like canola or vegetable)
1 cup (205 g) vegetable shortening, at room temperature

Whisk together the flour, oil, and shortening until smooth and apply with a pastry brush (or clean hand). Extra homemade pan release can be kept in a resealable jar for up to 2 months at room temperature.

HOW TO UNMOLD YOUR BUNDT PAN

It is easier to unmold your Bundt while it is still warm-ish. As the cake cools, the sugars in the cake are prone to stick to the sides of the pan. Follow this method for an easy release.

1. Remove the Bundt cake from the oven and allow to cool on a cooling rack for at least 15 minutes.
2. Place a wire cooling rack over the base of the cake (the part of the cake that is exposed in the pan facing up) and, grasping the pan and wire rack together, flip the whole thing over so that the pan is inverted and wire rack is the base. Place the wire rack over a dish towel (to catch crumbs and protect the work surface).
3. Before lifting the Bundt pan from the cake, give it a few bangs with your hand. Then remove the pan with the decorative side facing up.

HOW TO MELT CHOCOLATE OR CHOCOLATE *and* BUTTER

There are many recipes within this book that call for melted chocolate or melted butter and chocolate. The goal is to melt the ingredients but not heat them so much that they bubble, brown, or burn. It is much faster and easier to melt butter and chocolate that have already been cut into smaller pieces or chunks.

Use one of the two methods below:

Microwave Method

If you have a microwave, put your ingredients in a microwave-safe bowl and blast in 20-second increments at 50 percent power. Remove the bowl in between blasts and use a rubber spatula to stir and bring the ingredients together until melted, uniform, and combined. Note: If I am melting small amounts of butter or butter and chocolate, I often just place them in a glass measuring cup to make it easy to pour when needed.

Double-Boiler Method

Fill a medium saucepan with water. Place a steel mixing bowl over the pan so that it sits in the pan without touching the water. Add the ingredients to the steel bowl and set the pan over low heat. Agitate or stir the ingredients every 15 seconds until the ingredients are melted completely. Turn off the heat and remove the bowl from the pan and away from the steam coming off the pan. Stir until smooth.

HAPPINESS NOT HACKS

THE SMALL THINGS I DO IN THE KITCHEN THAT *Increase my Contentment* WITH MINIMAL EFFORT

I find "hacks" (life hacks, kitchen hacks, financial hacks, etc.) to be both an incredibly unpleasant term and concept. In practice, these viral (er . . . clickbait-y) "hacks" are supposed to either add a shortcut ("Peel garlic faster . . .") to an already simple task, or find a secondary use for a common household item ("Use your ironing board as a cooling rack . . ."). To me, most hacks feel like parlor tricks. Often, their usefulness is negligible. It is less about creating joy, and more about pumping out content.

In lieu of sharing a list of faster, easier, cheaper "hacks," I instead offer you a few things I practice that have brought me an easy endorphin boost as it relates to my baking life now.

MAGIC SHELL

My top summer delight is a soft-serve cone dipped in a chocolate coating that hardens upon contact with the ice cream. The hard chocolate crack giving way to a smooth vanilla custard is diabolically addictive. There are store-bought versions of this coating. Smucker's, the American food manufacturer, makes a product called "Magic Shell" that was ever-present in my mom's pantry. It is also quite easy to make your own chocolate shell. I do this frequently.

In a glass measuring cup, simply microwave about 1 cup (roughly 170 g) of dark chocolate chunks with 2 tablespoons of coconut oil (you can measure this either in solid or liquid form) on medium-high in short bursts (stirring in between each burst) until completely melted and smooth. Allow the mixture to cool for a few minutes before pouring it over the ice cream.

At this point, I rarely measure out the chocolate anymore. I just toss a few handfuls of chocolate into a glass measuring cup with the coconut oil, and I am always pleasantly surprised by the results. Sometimes the hard coating is satisfyingly chewy, and sometimes it "cracks." Both make me happy.

COOKIE HAPPY HOUR

Since leaving the professional bakery world, I have probably only ever baked off an entire recipe of cookies a handful of times. Instead, as mentioned throughout the book, I bake on demand for the warmest, freshest, widest assortment of cookies on a whim.

My refrigerator and freezer are full of pre-scooped cookie dough balls in various flavors. While most baked cookies have a three-day shelf life, it is impossible to beat a warm, fresh-from-the-oven cookie. And to be honest, a three-day-old cookie taste like a three-day-old cookie no matter how you frame it. One caveat: I don't do this with shortbread-style cookies.

Things to Note:

1. Fresh, pre-scooped cookie dough will generally last 1 week plus in the refrigerator and 1 month plus in the freezer.

2. For refrigerated dough, I preheat the oven, and immediately remove the balls from the refrigerator and place on the prepared baking sheets. By the time the oven heats up, the cookie dough is ready to go in the oven.

3. For frozen dough, I usually remove the dough from the freezer to room temperature (go ahead and just place on the baking sheets) 30 minutes before I start preheating the oven.

4. It is likely your refrigerated cookies will need another minute or two in the oven past the suggested bake time to account for the refrigeration.

FREEZE EVERYTHING

I used to feel a deep shame when I would freeze baked goods. It brought me to back to 1980s suburbia. A place where my family proudly utilized two deep chest freezers, placed—like trophies—at the head of our garage. The freezer was less a place of fresh food hibernation and more a way station for our store-bought ice cream, popsicles, and microwave dinners.

However, after living upstate with a sizable freezer (a massive upgrade from my New York City appliances), I am now embracing the wonders of fresh frozen food.

I freeze everything: Homemade sourdough bread, quartered and wrapped, is nearly indistinguishable from a same-day loaf. Most brownies direct from the freezer to mouth take on an almost bonbon-like consistency. Unfrosted cakes, wrapped properly, make same-day cake preparation a breeze.

You will not be thought of as bad baker for utilizing the freezer, but you will be a happier baker for making your life a little less stressful.

. . . OR GIVE IT AWAY

I inherited my Italian grandmother's gene for making an overabundance of food for even the smallest gathering. This usually means I am often left with a staggering amount of party leftovers. Yes, I could freeze all the excess cake, brownies, and pie, but I found that both my body and soul preferred if I gave it away to guests or nearby neighbors. I suggest making the "leftovers" a bit more presentable. Invest in a sleeve of reusable, recyclable cardboard takeaway packs—no one wants a mystery hunk wrapped in tinfoil, and I promise you, no one wants to return your plastic food storage.

EVERYTHING GETS WHIPPED CREAM

Fresh whipped cream is a mood. I find it incredibly pleasing to make. It is a low effort add-on to any gathering and highly appreciated by guests. Here is the thing about whipped cream. You don't really need a specific reason to make it. I mean, yes, make it for hot chocolate or as an accompaniment to strawberries or rich dark chocolate torte, but also just make it. Make it for breakfasts (dress up pancakes, waffles, even muffins), after lunch (dollop in your espresso, plop on your cookies and brownies), or any dinner party dessert.

These days I very rarely measure anything out. I usually just put a few good pours (1 cup/240 ml) of whipped cream in a chilled metal bowl and whisk* it vigorously until soft peaks form before adding a teaspoon of extract (usually vanilla, but go off on any flavor) and maybe a tablespoon or two of confectioners' sugar to help it stabilize and hold its form a bit longer. Then, I keep whisking until gorgeous medium peaks form. Hand out spoons to your guests to enjoy.

*Yes, you can absolutely put this on a stand mixer and beat it up in no time, but I do not always feel like dragging my mixer out for this purpose. Besides, I actually enjoy doing this by hand.

TOP 5 ESSENTIAL (AND *Quick* AND *Easy*)

SURE THING DESSERTS

CHOOSE YOUR OWN *Adventure* CHOCOLATE CHIP COOKIES

I have learned a few things about chocolate chip cookies after making, quite literally, hundreds of variations over the years. One, there are barely perceptible, ever-so-slight incremental differences between a chocolate chip cookie that takes twenty minutes to throw together and one that takes three days. (Unless you are trying to win an award, go with quicker and easier.) Two, no matter the recipe, you should always use a good-quality chocolate chip, but it is always preferable to use a chocolate chunk (I like to mix equal portions milk and dark chunks). Three, while most cookies—wrapped tightly—are acceptable up to three days after baking, they are much better on the day they are baked. Keep freshly scooped dough balls in the fridge or freezer and bake on demand.

My entire chocolate-chip-cookie life changed when I stumbled upon Tara O'Brady's recipe. For years, I have been creaming butter and sugar in my stand mixer (and cleaning the stand mixer thereafter) for myself, for soon-to-arrive guests, for neighbors, and for parties. My mixer got a lot of use. However, Tara's recipe did away with the mixer altogether by utilizing melted butter. This was a game changer. You could save time without sacrificing quality. And while I do have an affinity for my mixer, I must be honest, I have not brought it out to make a chocolate chip cookie in years. Both of the following recipes are riffs on Tara's classic chocolate chip recipe, and both come together quickly and without excess equipment.

FAST, NO-FUSS, DELICIOUS *Classic* CHOCOLATE CHIP

MAKES 24 TO 30 COOKIES, DEPENDING ON SCOOP SIZE

TL/DR: This is, perhaps, the only chocolate chip cookie recipe you will need. It deserves five stars. The dough comes together in ten minutes—especially if you are weighing the ingredients—and does not require a mixer. It tastes every bit as good as those recipes that require funny ingredients and extra equipment.

- 8 ounces (16 tablespoons / 225 g) unsalted butter, cut into ½-inch cubes
- 3 cups (375 g) all-purpose flour
- 1¼ teaspoons baking powder
- 1 teaspoon baking soda
- 1 teaspoon kosher salt
- 1 cup packed (220 g) light brown sugar
- ¾ cup (150 g) granulated sugar
- 2 large eggs
- 1 tablespoon pure vanilla extract
- 6 ounces (170 g) dark chocolate, 60 to 70 percent cacao, coarsely chopped
- 6 ounces (170 g) milk chocolate, coarsely chopped
- Flake sea salt, such as Maldon, for topping

Melt the butter in a microwave or over low heat in a saucepan until just melted, not browned.

In a large bowl, whisk together the flour, baking powder, baking soda, and salt.

In a separate large mixing bowl, combine the brown and granulated sugars and pour in the melted butter. Whisk the mixture vigorously until smooth. Add the eggs, one at a time, until combined. Whisk in the vanilla.

Pour the dry ingredients into the egg mixture and use a spatula to bring the mixture together—almost as if you were folding in dry ingredients for a cake batter. Once the mixture is mostly uniform, stir in the dark and milk chocolate chunks. Cover the bowl and place in the refrigerator while you preheat the oven.

Preheat the oven to 350°F (180°C) and line two half sheet baking pans with parchment paper. Once your oven heats up, use a medium ice-cream scoop with a release mechanism (or a small spoon and your hands) to form balls (each 2 to 3 heaping tablespoons) and place on the prepared cookie sheet about 2 inches (5 cm) apart. Sprinkle the top of each cookie with a few flakes of sea salt.

Bake until the edges of the cookies are golden brown or start to darken, 11 to 13 minutes. If baking two sheet pans worth of cookies at the same time, it is a good idea to rotate the pans bottom to top to ensure an equal consistency. Bang the pan on the counter right before letting the cookies cool. Cool the cookies directly on the pan before serving, but obviously feel free to serve slightly warm.

The cookies can be stored in an airtight container for up to 3 days.

Chewy MALT CHOCOLATE CHIP

MAKES 24 TO 30 COOKIES, DEPENDING ON SCOOP SIZE

By way of the bread flour and a slight recalibrating of the sugars, this is a slightly chewier take on the classic chocolate chip. The malted milk powder adds a pleasant hint of nuttiness and warmth. If the classic chocolate chip is my summer/spring go-to, this one is my fall/winter favorite.

8 ounces (16 tablespoons / 225 g) unsalted butter, cut into ½-inch cubes

3 cups (375 g) bread flour

3 tablespoons malted milk powder

1¼ teaspoons baking powder

1 teaspoon baking soda

1 teaspoon kosher salt

1¼ cups packed (275 g) light brown sugar

½ cup (105 g) granulated sugar

2 large eggs

1 tablespoon pure vanilla extract

6 ounces (170 g) dark chocolate, 60 to 75 percent cacao, coarsely chopped

6 ounces (170 g) milk chocolate, coarsely chopped

Flake sea salt, such as Maldon, for topping

Melt the butter in a microwave or in a saucepan over low heat until just melted, not browned.

In a large bowl, whisk together the flour, malted milk powder, baking powder, baking soda, and salt.

In a separate large mixing bowl, combine the brown sugar and granulated sugar and pour in the melted butter. Whisk the mixture vigorously until smooth. Add the eggs, one at a time, until combined. Whisk in the vanilla.

Pour the dry ingredients into the egg mixture and use a spatula to bring the mixture together—almost as if you were folding in dry ingredients for a cake batter. Once the mixture is mostly uniform, stir in the dark and milk chocolate chunks. Cover the bowl and place in the refrigerator while you preheat the oven.

Preheat the oven to 350°F (180°C) and line two half sheet baking pans with parchment paper. Once the oven heats up, use a medium ice-cream scoop with a release mechanism (or a small spoon and your hands) to form balls of 2 to 3 heaping tablespoons. Place on the prepared cookie sheet about 2 inches (5 cm) apart. Sprinkle the top of each cookie with a few flakes of sea salt.

Bake for 11 to 13 minutes, until the edges of the cookies are golden brown or start to darken. Bang the pan on the counter right before letting the cookies cool. Cool the cookies directly on the pan before serving, but obviously feel free to serve slightly warm.

The cookies can be stored in an airtight container for up to 3 days.

SURE THING NOTE

Yes, you can use any combo of chocolate you like, but I really think you will be happier with chopped chocolate (I like using Valrhona fèves) as opposed to chocolate chips. I really like Valrhona's Jivara 40 percent milk chocolate in this recipe, as it goes well with the warmth of the malt powder.

Classic BROWNIE (REDUX)

MAKES 16 BROWNIES

The original version of this brownie recipe essentially launched Baked, a Brooklyn-based bakery I co-founded. The brownie recipe evolved from a dear friend, Lesli Flick, and went on to garner praise from Oprah (it was one of her favorite things), Martha Stewart, and dozens of media outlets and consumers alike only six months after the bakery opened. It was a bit intense and all at once, but our brownie did deserve it. Shamefully, brownies never quite get the same attention as chocolate chip cookies or funky shaped croissants, so I was happy to see this simple dessert get some outsize praise.

Given that the original recipe is iconic, I made only minor tweaks. First, I scaled it down to fit a smaller pan for smaller occasions. Second, I skipped the separate whisking of dry ingredients in an effort to streamline the process and eliminate a bowl. Finally, I removed one egg from the original recipe to lean more into the fudgy brownie texture. The result: It is every bit as chocolate forward and heavenly as the one that changed our bakery overnight.

- 6 ounces (170 g) dark chocolate (about 70 percent cacao)
- 4 ounces (8 tablespoons / 115 g) unsalted butter
- ¾ cup (150 g) granulated sugar
- ¼ cup packed (55 g) light brown sugar
- 2 large eggs, at room temperature
- 2 teaspoons pure vanilla extract
- ¾ cup (95 g) all-purpose flour
- 1 tablespoon unsweetened Dutch-process cocoa powder
- 1 teaspoon kosher salt
- ½ teaspoon espresso powder

Preheat the oven to 350°F (180°C) and position a rack in the center. Butter the sides and bottom of a light-colored metal 8-inch (20-cm) square pan. Line with parchment paper so that it overhangs by about 1 inch (2.5 cm) on two sides of the pan. Butter the paper.

Melt the chocolate and butter together using the microwave or double-boiler method (see page 33). Stir occasionally, until the chocolate and butter are completely melted, smooth, and combined. Remove from the heat and add both the granulated and brown sugars. Whisk until completely combined, about 1 minute. The mixture will look a bit sandy, which is fine. Wait about 5 minutes, or until the mixture is near room temperature (you don't want to cook your egg).

Add the eggs and vanilla to the mixture and whisk until just combined. Do not overbeat the batter.

recipe continues next page

Sprinkle the flour, cocoa powder, salt, and espresso powder over the chocolate mixture. Use a spatula to fold the mixture into the chocolate until just a bit of flour mixture is visible. Pour the batter into the prepared pan and smooth the top.

Bake until a toothpick inserted into the center of the brownies comes out with a few moist crumbs sticking to it, about 30 minutes (but it might be wise to start checking the brownies at the 25-minute mark).

Remove from the oven, place on a cooling rack, and let the brownies cool completely. Use a small paring knife to release the brownies from the sides of the pan and pull straight up on the parchment to remove. Cut and serve.

The brownies will keep in an airtight container at room temperature for up to 3 days. The brownies also freeze wonderfully and can be eaten directly from the freezer, or thaw completely (for about 45 minutes at room temperature) before serving.

SURE THING NOTE

Admittedly, I have made these brownies without either the espresso powder (I realized I didn't have any in the house) or the cocoa powder (I completely forgot this ingredient in a mad rush of baking) or both and the difference in the final product and taste is very slight. Yes, you can skip either one or both of these ingredients, and you will still be very pleased; but if you do have both items in the cupboard, you might as well use them. The espresso powder cuts the sweetness ever so slightly, and the cocoa powder adds a welcome, almost smoky element.

YELLOW PICNIC *Party* CAKE

SERVES 16

Look, everyone should have a quick and tasty yellow cake recipe in their back pocket. It doesn't have to be fancy or frilly or have many tiers, but it should be something you feel comfortable throwing together for whatever casual occasion calls. But why is it a picnic party cake? No good reason really, other than that I tend to bake this for outdoor events (like barbecues, pool parties, picnics), and it transports well in the baking pan. It's a fuss-free dopamine hit. The cake itself is a single layer stand-up moist yellow sponge, and it is topped with an old-school vanilla-forward frosting that has very few haters. It's reminiscent of both what your mom used to make from a box as well as what your favorite bakery serves by the slice. Dress it up with a few sprinkles or chocolate bits and make it your signature picnic staple.

FOR THE CAKE:

- 1½ cups (190 g) all-purpose flour
- 1 teaspoon cornstarch
- 1½ teaspoons baking powder
- ½ teaspoon baking soda
- ½ teaspoon kosher salt
- 1 cup (200 g) granulated sugar
- 4 ounces (8 tablespoons / 115 g) unsalted butter, softened, cut into ½-inch cubes
- 1 tablespoon vegetable oil
- 2 large eggs
- 1 egg yolk
- 1 teaspoon pure vanilla extract
- ½ cup (120 g) sour cream
- ½ cup (120 ml) whole milk

MAKE THE CAKE

Preheat the oven to 350°F (180°C) and position a rack in the center. Butter the sides and bottom of a light-colored metal 8-inch (20-cm) square pan. Line the bottom with parchment paper and butter the paper.

In the bowl of a stand mixer fitted with the paddle attachment, mix together the flour, cornstarch, baking powder, baking soda, salt, and granulated sugar until combined. Add the butter and oil and beat on medium speed until the mixture looks like a sandy, coarse cornmeal and no visible butter clumps remain.

Add the eggs, egg yolk, and vanilla and beat on medium speed until the mixture is thick and smooth. Add the sour cream and turn the mixer to its slowest setting. Slowly stream in the milk, stopping the mixer one or two times to scrape the sides and bottom of the mixing bowl, then increase the speed to medium and beat until the mixture is smooth and uniform. Pour the mixture into the prepared pan and smooth the top.

Bake for 32 to 37 minutes, until a toothpick comes out clean and the cake is golden. Place the pan on a wire rack and let the cake cool before frosting.

recipe continues next page

FOR THE VANILLA FROSTING:

- 4 ounces (8 tablespoons / 115 g) unsalted butter, softened, cut into ½-inch cubes
- 2 cups (250 g) confectioners' sugar, plus more as needed
- 2 tablespoons heavy cream
- 1 teaspoon vanilla bean paste or pure vanilla extract
- Pinch salt
- 3 tablespoons chocolate or rainbow sprinkles for topping

MAKE THE VANILLA FROSTING

In the bowl of a stand mixer fitted with the paddle attachment, beat the softened butter on medium speed until very smooth and creamy, 2 to 3 minutes. Add the confectioners' sugar and 1 tablespoon of the heavy cream and beat until combined. Add the vanilla, salt, and the additional tablespoon of heavy cream and beat until thick but spreadable. If the frosting seems too loose, add additional confectioners' sugar, 1 tablespoon at a time, until it becomes thicker.

ASSEMBLE THE CAKE

Once the cake is completely cool, transfer it to a platter if desired (it is much easier to cut and serve out of the pan). With an offset spatula, spread the frosting on the cake into an even layer and top with sprinkles. I like to refrigerate the cake for 10 to 15 minutes to set the cake and frosting before serving, but it is not necessary.

The cake will keep in an airtight container at room temperature for up to 3 days.

SURE THING NOTE

This cake uses a reverse creaming method that not only produces a lighter crumb (it is hard to overbeat the cake when using this method) but, just as importantly, is slightly faster to pull together (okay, maybe it only saves a few minutes max, but if you make this cake a hundred times that is nearly 250 minutes you will get back in your life).

LEMON *Drizzle* CAKE (SCOTTISH VERSION)

SERVES 8 TO 10

With good reason, lemon loaf cake is very popular in Scotland, even if the entire population refers to this type of tea cake as lemon drizzle cake regardless of how the glaze is applied—whether it be a wee drizzle or a cement-like glaze. I know this because my partner is from Scotland, and we make frequent trips back to his homeland where I tend to double down on all the lemon loaf cakes the country has to offer.

I happen to like all manner of lemon cakes—Bundt, loaf, with or without poppy seeds—so I had a difficult time picking my favorite "sure thing" recipe for inclusion in this book. In the end, I chose a classic recipe and attempted to simplify it so you will make it frequently. It is extremely lemony and it has the most pleasant crumb—not too heavy nor too light. I thought a loaf format would be more applicable to daily life, whereas a Bundt always feels like a "party" recipe. I ditched the usual "lemon soak" step in favor of a dash of lemon extract. It's a shortcut that works. By all means, add that lemon drizzle glaze however you see fit. I am from the more-is-more camp, but you can go with a dainty application, if you so desire.

FOR THE LEMON LOAF CAKE:

1½ cups (190 g) all-purpose flour

1½ teaspoons baking powder

½ teaspoon kosher salt

½ cup (115 g) sour cream

¼ cup (60 g) fresh lemon juice

3 tablespoons vegetable oil

1 cup (200 g) granulated sugar

Freshly grated zest of 3 lemons

4 ounces (8 tablespoons / 115 g) unsalted butter, softened, cut into ½-inch cubes

3 large eggs, at room temperature

1 teaspoon pure vanilla extract

1 teaspoon lemon extract

MAKE THE LEMON LOAF CAKE

Preheat the oven to 350°F (180°C). Spray the sides and bottom of one (9 by 5 by 3-inch / 23 by 13 by 7.5-cm) loaf pan with nonstick baking spray. Line with parchment paper so it overhangs by about 1 inch (2.5 cm) on the two long sides. Spray the paper.

In a medium bowl, whisk together the flour, baking powder, and salt. Set aside.

In a glass measuring cup or small bowl, whisk together the sour cream, lemon juice, and oil. Set aside.

In the bowl of a stand mixer, combine the granulated sugar and lemon zest. Use your fingers to rub the zest into the sugar until the mixture looks somewhat uniform and lemony in color.

recipe continues next page

SURE THING NOTE

The addition of the lemon extract might seem arbitrary (after all it is only 1 teaspoon), but it really coaxes a pleasant lemony taste to the forefront without a lot of extra work. Look for "pure" lemon extract in the same section of the grocery store as vanilla extract.

FOR THE LEMON "DRIZZLE" GLAZE:

1 tablespoon fresh lemon juice

Freshly grated zest of 1 lemon

1 tablespoon heavy cream, plus more as needed

¾ cup (95 g) confectioners' sugar, plus more as needed

Pinch kosher salt

Place the bowl on the stand mixer fitted with the paddle attachment. Add the butter to the sugar and beat on medium speed until light and creamy, about 3 minutes. Scrape down the sides and bottom of the bowl and add the eggs, one at a time, beating well after each addition. Add the vanilla and lemon extracts and beat again for 30 seconds.

Add the flour mixture in three parts, alternating with the sour cream mixture, beginning and ending with the flour mixture. Beat each addition gently on the lowest speed to combine. Do not overmix.

Pour the batter into the prepared loaf pan and smooth the top. Tap the pan gently on the counter to remove any air bubbles.

Bake for 45 to 55 minutes, until a toothpick inserted into the center comes out clean, and the top is golden brown.

Remove the cake from the oven and let cool in the pan for about 20 minutes. Use a small paring knife to help release the lemon loaf from the sides of the pan and pull up on the parchment overhang to remove the loaf. Transfer to a wire cooling rack. Place the cooling rack over a sheet pan. This will help to catch excess glaze (for easier cleanup) in the next step.

MAKE THE LEMON "DRIZZLE" GLAZE

When the cake is nearly cool, use a toothpick to poke several holes all over each loaf.

In a small bowl, whisk together the lemon juice, lemon zest, heavy cream, confectioners' sugar, and salt until smooth. The mixture should be thick but pourable. If the mixture seems too thin, add more confectioners' sugar, 1 tablespoon at a time, until you reach the desired consistency. Alternatively, if the icing looks too thick, add more heavy cream, a teaspoon at a time, until it is pourable.

Pour the lemon drizzle glaze over the loaf, allowing it to soak in. Allow the glaze to set before serving.

Leftover lemon loaf, when wrapped tightly at room temperature, will last for up to 3 days.

LEMON *Poppy Seed* LOAF AND GLAZE

For me, the poppy seeds add a nice visual, but I am not sure they add much in the taste department. I truly love the way the poppy seeds speckle the loaf and especially the glaze.

To turn this loaf into a poppy seed loaf, simply add 2 tablespoons of poppy seeds with the vanilla and lemon extracts in the loaf cake. Whisk 1 teaspoon of poppy seeds into the glaze once you reach a desired consistency.

A POSH CHOCOLATE CAKE

SERVES 8 TO 12

Well before I co-founded a bakery, I was making this rather posh, simple cake for various evening gatherings and get-togethers. While minimal in appearance, the cake suggests an effortless cool. It is extremely rich and chocolaty and dense, but it is not completely fudge-like because the tiny bit of flour gives it enough body to hold its form. Serve solo, dusted in confectioners' sugar, or alongside a fluffy dollop of whipped cream or indulgent scoop of gelato.

I should note the origins of this recipe are derived from Nick Malgieri's grand-maman's cake recipe from his workhorse of a book, *Chocolate*. That book, covering a great deal of chocolate recipes, was the impetus for my career change and just holding it in my hands brings me a great deal of joy.

8 ounces (225 g) dark chocolate (about 70 percent cacao), coarsely chopped

4 large eggs, at room temperature

1 cup (200 g) granulated sugar

5 ounces (10 tablespoons / 150 g) unsalted butter, softened, cut into ½-inch chunks

¾ cup (95 g) all-purpose flour

Confectioners' sugar for dusting

1 pint (475 ml) vanilla gelato (optional)

Melt the chocolate until smooth using either the double-boiler method or microwave method on page 33. Set aside to cool.

Preheat the oven to 350°F (180°C) and position a rack in the center. Lightly spray a 9-inch (23-cm) springform pan with nonstick baking spray. Line the bottom of the pan with parchment paper and lightly spray the paper and sides of the pan.

In the bowl of a stand mixer fitted with the whisk attachment, beat the eggs and sugar on medium-high speed for about 4 minutes, until the mixture is very pale and light in color. Add the butter and whip for 1 minute on medium speed. Add the chocolate and whip on medium speed until both the butter and the chocolate are completely incorporated.

Remove the bowl from the mixer, add the flour, and fold it in gently using a rubber spatula until just combined. Scrape the batter into the prepared pan and smooth the top with an offset spatula.

Bake the cake for 25 to 30 minutes, until the sides are set and the middle does not jiggle. If you are using a toothpick to test, it should still be very moist in the center, but not underdone.

recipe continues next page

SURE THING NOTE

If you do not have a springform pan handy, you can absolutely bake this cake in a regular 9-inch (23-cm) round pan. But note, because this cake is a bit delicate, you could end up with a few broken bits around the edges and some cooling rack marks on top of the cake from inverting the cake to get it out and upright. Truly not the end of the world, and you can easily cover up tiny mistakes with a dusting of confectioners' sugar.

Allow to cool for 20 minutes in the pan on the cooling rack, then release the sides of the springform and allow to cool completely. Place the cake in the refrigerator for about 30 minutes or up to 3 hours to firm up. Use a small offset spatula to pry the cake from the bottom of the springform and remove the parchment paper before placing it on a serving dish and dusting with confectioners' sugar. Serve alongside the gelato, if using.

Note: The cake in the photo is covered in gelato as an optional "frosting." To achieve the same effect, scoop a pint of ice cream into the bowl of a stand mixer fitted with the paddle attachment and beat on high until smooth but still firm. Spoon onto the cake and "frost" to cover before placing the cake in the freezer for the ice cream layer to set—about 15 minutes—before serving.

The cake will keep up to 3 days (obviously, without the ice cream "frosting") in an airtight container at room temperature, but I prefer the texture and coolness of this cake when refrigerated (also in an airtight container).

A POSH *Vegan* CHOCOLATE CAKE

MAKES ONE 9-INCH LAYER

This is a simple vegan version of my favorite Posh Chocolate Cake (page 56). Like the Posh Chocolate Cake, I usually leave it unadorned, but it is a great canvas for any and all vegan sauces, syrups, and frostings.

- 1½ (180 g) cups all-purpose flour
- 1 cup (198 g) granulated sugar
- ⅓ cup (28 g) unsweetened cocoa powder, sifted
- 1 teaspoon baking powder
- ½ teaspoon fine sea salt (kosher salt will do)
- 1 cup (240 ml) hot black coffee
- ¾ cup (177 ml) extra-virgin olive oil
- 2 teaspoons pure vanilla extract
- 3 ounces (85 g) vegan dark chocolate, melted and slightly cooled
- 1 tablespoon apple cider vinegar
- ½ teaspoon baking soda

Preheat the oven to 350°F (180°C) and position a rack in the center. Lightly spray a 9 by 2-inch (23 by 5-cm) round cake pan with nonstick cooking spray. Line the pan with parchment paper and lightly spray the parchment and sides of the pan.

In a medium to large mixing bowl, whisk together the flour, sugar, cocoa powder, baking powder, and salt until well combined.

Make a well in the center of the dry ingredients. Pour in the coffee, olive oil, vanilla, and melted chocolate. Using a rubber spatula, fold the ingredients together until the batter is smooth.

In a small glass measuring cup, stir together the apple cider vinegar and baking soda. It will bubble up. Once all the baking soda is dissolved (this will happen quickly) pour it over the batter and fold in gently until the batter is uniform.

Pour the batter into the prepared cake pan and bake for 32 to 36 minutes, or until a toothpick inserted into the center comes out clean.

Allow to cool completely before removing from the pan and serving.

The cake will keep up to 3 days in an airtight container at room temperature.

BARS AND BROWNIES

(AND *a Crisp*)

Brown Butter SNICKERDOODLE BARS

MAKES 16 SMALL BARS

If I had to rank cookies in terms of my top varieties, snickerdoodles would not be far behind my beloved first-place contender, chocolate chip cookies. They are fairly universal (that is, no one is trying to reinvent the wheel thankfully), almost always pleasing, and really easy to make. And of course, they also work really well as a bar. When a snickerdoodle becomes a bar, it floats in the space between blondie and sugar cookie in that it makes the loveliest afternoon snack, but it also cries out to be paired with a cup of coffee or tea. This recipe is straightforward. Expect a pop of cinnamon and a cookie with an almost cake-like texture. It has all the hallmarks of a favorite bake sale treat.

FOR THE BARS:

5 ounces (10 tablespoons / 150 g) unsalted butter, cut into ½-inch cubes

1¾ cups (220 g) all-purpose flour

½ teaspoon cream of tartar

½ teaspoon kosher salt

½ teaspoon baking soda

¼ teaspoon baking powder

½ teaspoon ground cinnamon

¾ cup (150 g) granulated sugar

¼ cup packed (55 g) light brown sugar

1 teaspoon pure vanilla extract

1 large egg

1 egg yolk

FOR THE TOPPING:

2 tablespoons granulated sugar

½ teaspoon ground cinnamon

1 tablespoon unsalted butter, melted

MAKE THE BARS

Preheat the oven to 350°F (180°C) and position a rack in the center. Butter the sides and bottom of a light-colored metal 8-inch (20-cm) square pan. Line with parchment paper so that it overhangs by about 1 inch (2.5 cm) on two sides of the pan. Butter the paper.

Put the butter in a small saucepan over medium-high heat and cook, swirling the pan occasionally, until the foam subsides and the butter turns a light nut-brown, 3 to 4 minutes; watch carefully so it does not burn. Remove from the heat and set aside to cool while you prepare the rest of the recipe.

In a medium bowl, whisk together the flour, cream of tartar, salt, baking soda, baking powder, and cinnamon.

In a separate medium bowl, combine the granulated and brown sugars. Pour the cooled browned butter over the sugars and whisk until moistened. Add the vanilla and whisk a few more times. Add the egg and egg yolk and whisk until incorporated and the batter is uniform. Add the dry ingredients all at once and fold, with a rubber spatula, until combined.

SURE THING NOTE

I tested this bar with several different toppings, and while all were good, they all distracted from the snickerdoodle vibe. However, adding about 2 tablespoons of crushed almonds to the cinnamon sugar was a crowd-pleaser if you want to give that a whirl.

Turn the dough out into the prepared pan and quickly press it into an even layer with the back of a flat spatula.

Bake for 26 to 28 minutes, until the edges are set and the middle is puffy. Remove from the oven and let cool for about 10 minutes while you make the topping.

MAKE THE TOPPING

In a small bowl, stir together the granulated sugar and cinnamon. Brush the top of the bars with the melted butter and sprinkle the cinnamon-sugar mixture over. Let cool completely.

Use a small paring knife to release the bars from the sides of the pan and pull straight up on the parchment to remove. Cut and serve.

The bars can be kept at room temperature, tightly covered, for up to 3 days.

APPLE *Brandy* BARS

MAKES ABOUT 12 BARS OR 16 SMALL BARS

I live in the Hudson Valley, surrounded by apple orchards with a pick-your-own carnival-like atmosphere: throngs of people, flowing apple cider, fresh donuts, and corn mazes. I fall hard for these sorts of enterprises, but I almost always pick too many apples. I return with buckets and bags of gorgeous apples—wholly losing myself in the spirit of the orchard experience. Yet I almost never reach for an apple as a snack. I prefer apples that are cored and diced and covered in butter and sugar. This is a simple bar recipe designed to put excess apples to a better use. The crumble—excessively easy to throw together—works overtime as both a base and a topping, and the apple mixture is a cinch minus the somewhat annoying part of peeling and diving the apples. The final result is not quite as delicate as grandma's apple pie, but it is pretty spectacular and a lot easier to make.

FOR THE FILLING:

- 1½ pounds (680 g) green apples (around 5 regular-size), peeled and diced into ½-inch cubes
- 3 tablespoons unsalted butter
- 2 tablespoons granulated sugar
- 2 tablespoons light brown sugar
- 2 teaspoons cornstarch
- ⅛ teaspoon cinnamon
- ¼ teaspoon kosher salt
- 1½ tablespoons brandy or whiskey

FOR THE CRUMBLE:

- 1½ cups (190 g) all-purpose flour
- ⅔ cup (70 g) old-fashioned rolled oats
- ¾ cup packed (165 g) light brown sugar
- ½ teaspoon ground cinnamon
- ½ teaspoon kosher salt
- 6 ounces (12 tablespoons / 170 g) unsalted butter, cold, cut into ½-inch cubes

PREPARE THE FILLING

Combine the apples, butter, granulated and brown sugars, cornstarch, cinnamon, and salt in a medium-size pot. Stir the mixture together and cook over medium heat, stirring every few minutes, until the apples are softened but still holding their shape, and the mixture has reduced and developed a slight sauciness, 10 to 12 minutes. Remove from the heat and stir in the brandy. Set aside until fully cooled, about 30 minutes.

Preheat the oven to 350°F (180°C) and position a rack in the center. Butter the sides and bottom of a light-colored metal 8-inch (20-cm) square pan. Line with parchment paper so that it overhangs by about 1 inch (2.5 cm) on two sides of the pan. Butter the paper.

ASSEMBLE THE APPLE CRUMBLE

In a medium bowl, stir together the flour, oats, brown sugar, cinnamon, and salt. Add the cold, cubed butter. Use your fingertips to rub the butter evenly into the flour mixture until the butter is pea-size.

recipe continues next page

SURE THING NOTES

If you can, go with green apples for two reasons: They are less sweet than other varieties, and they don't get as mushy when baked. Also, while the bars can last 3 days when stored properly, I really encourage you to eat them sooner, as the crumble (like a pie crust) will get progressively soggier with time. They are still delicious, but the snap of the crumble dissipates. If you are eating these a day or two after making, I suggest heating these up in a 200°F (95°C) oven for 5 to 10 minutes to "crisp" up the bars before serving.

Spread about half the crumble into the prepared pan and use the flat side of an offset spatula to gently press into an even layer. Top the crumb layer with the apple mixture. Sprinkle the remaining crumble mixture in an even layer over the apple mixture.

Bake for 37 to 45 minutes, until the top is browned and the edges are crisp—the crispier the better. Wait until the bars are completely cool before slicing for a cleaner slice. If you slice while warm, the bars will taste great but might fall apart. Use a small paring knife to release the bars from the sides of the pan and pull straight up on the parchment to remove.

The bars can be kept at room temperature, tightly covered, for up to 3 days.

Pear BLUEBERRY CRISP

SERVES 8 TO 10

In my opinion, crisps only need to achieve two goals to be considered winners. One, they have to be easy to throw together—no food processors or mixers, and the fewer dirty bowls the better. Two, they should be served warm. I have yet to meet a lackluster crisp—even one that has gone off the rails—if it is served warm and with ice cream. This crisp happens to be a favorite combo. The pears and blueberries are coated in a hint of fall spices and baked until warm and bubbling perfection. My suggestion: Toss it in the oven near the end of any gathering and serve buffet-style with ice cream and caramel (see page 81). Life is hard sometimes. Dessert shouldn't be.

FOR THE PEAR BLUEBERRY FILLING:

- 2½ pounds (1.1 kg) pears (4 to 5 large pears)
- 1 cup (190 g) blueberries (fresh or frozen)
- ¼ cup (50 g) granulated sugar
- 2 teaspoons cornstarch
- 2 tablespoons fresh lemon juice
- ½ teaspoon kosher salt
- 1 tablespoon grated fresh ginger, or ½ teaspoon dried ground ginger
- 1 teaspoon ground cinnamon
- ¼ teaspoon ground nutmeg

FOR THE OAT TOPPING:

- 1 cup (90 g) old-fashioned rolled oats
- ⅓ cup (40 g) all-pupose flour
- 2 tablespoons granulated sugar
- ¼ cup firmly packed (55 g) light brown sugar
- ¼ teaspoon ground cinnamon
- ¼ teaspoon kosher salt
- 4 ounces (8 tablespoons / 115 g) cold unsalted butter, cut into ½-inch cubes

Preheat the oven to 375°F (190°C) and position a rack near the center of the oven. Generously butter the sides and bottom of a 10-inch (25-cm) cast-iron skillet or similar size baking dish (this can be a 10-inch / 25-cm cake pan or any baking vessel about this size—like your favorite oval baking dish—because this recipe is fairly flexible).

MAKE THE PEAR BLUEBERRY FILLING

Peel the pears (or don't!), core, and cut into ¼-inch-thick (6-mm) slices.

In a large bowl, measure out 6 cups (1.4 L) sliced pears. Add the blueberries, sugar, and cornstarch and toss together with a large spoon. Add the lemon juice, salt, ginger, cinnamon, and nutmeg and toss gently until combined. Pour the fruit mixture into the prepared pan.

MAKE THE OAT TOPPING

In a medium bowl, whisk together the oats, flour, granulated and brown sugars, cinnamon, and salt. Add the cold, cubed butter. Break the butter into the dry mixture with a pastry cutter or by pinching it between your fingertips. Continue until the mixture forms large clumps. Sprinkle the topping over the pears in an even layer.

recipe continues next page

SURE THING NOTES

If you are lucky enough to have fresh blueberries on hand, they will work beautifully in this recipe, but frozen blueberries are fine—just note that your bake time might be a tad bit longer. Also, I have tested this crisp with both Bosc and Bartlett pears, and while each has its merits, a medium-ripe Bosc really shines here. Bosc pears do not change color as they ripen, but when they are ripe, the stem end will give slightly if pressed.

Bake for 45 to 55 minutes, until the top is bubbling and browned. Remove from the oven, place the pan on a cooling rack, and allow to cool slightly. Serve the crisp warm, with vanilla ice cream, if you like.

Wrap and refrigerate any leftover crisp for up to 3 days. To reheat, let the crisp come to room temperature, then rewarm it in a 300°F (150°C) oven for 15 to 20 minutes.

LEMON *Cheesecake* BARS WITH CHERRY SAUCE

MAKES 16 BARS

I am easily swayed by anything cream cheese adjacent. Cream cheese frosting? Yes, please. Cheesecake brownies? I want them all. Cheesecake ice cream? My idea of heaven. But classic and simple cheesecake bars are perhaps the best way to experience the joys of cream cheese. While this recipe hews closely to all manner of other cheesecake bar recipes out there (why mess with a classic?), I encourage you to either push the vanilla or lemon flavor to your limit. For these bars, I offer a balance of both, but I would also be happy to see you lean heavier on one flavor or the other. Also, it must be said that the cheesecake bars are perfect in their au naturel state, and I rarely make the cherry sauce accompaniment unless I am serving these bars for a dinner party or other special event. They are nearly perfect on their own, but the sauce adds a nice balance and a few of my friends actually request it.

FOR THE GRAHAM CRACKER CRUST:

- 1⅓ cups (150 g) graham cracker crumbs
- ¼ cup (50 g) granulated sugar
- ¼ teaspoon kosher salt
- 2½ ounces (5 tablespoons / 70 g) unsalted butter, melted

FOR THE SOUR CREAM TOPPING:

- ¾ cup (180 g) sour cream
- 3 tablespoons granulated sugar
- ½ teaspoon pure vanilla extract

MAKE THE GRAHAM CRACKER CRUST

Preheat the oven to 350°F (180°C) and position a rack in the center. Butter the sides and bottom of a light-colored metal 8-inch (20-cm) square pan. Line with parchment paper so that it overhangs by about 1 inch (2.5 cm) on two sides of the pan. Butter the paper.

In a small bowl, combine the graham cracker crumbs, sugar, and salt. Stir to blend, then add the melted butter and stir until the mixture is wet and well mixed. Turn the mixture out into the prepared pan and press it into an even layer. Bake for 10 to 12 minutes, until fragrant (visually it won't look much different). Set aside.

MAKE THE SOUR CREAM TOPPING

In a small bowl, whisk together the sour cream, sugar, and vanilla until smooth. Set aside.

recipe continues next page

SURE THING NOTE

While the bars are quite sturdy, they will absolutely cut more cleanly if you run the knife under hot water in between each slice. Also, if you want to make the cherry sauce using fresh cherries, adjust the cook time from 5 to 7 minutes down to 2 to 3 minutes. Finally, I generally chop half of the cherries before cooking the sauce to add texture, but it is entirely unnecessary and fully based on preference.

FOR THE CREAM CHEESE FILLING:

2 (8-ounce / 225 g) packages cream cheese, at room temperature

¼ cup (60 g) sour cream, at room temperature

1 cup (200 g) granulated sugar

¼ teaspoon kosher salt

1½ teaspoons pure vanilla extract

3 tablespoons fresh lemon juice

Freshly grated zest of 1 lemon

3 large eggs, at room temperature

FOR THE CHERRY SAUCE:

1½ cups (240 g) frozen pitted sweet cherries

2 tablespoons water

2 teaspoons fresh lemon juice

1 teaspoon cornstarch

2 tablespoons granulated sugar

MAKE THE CREAM CHEESE FILLING

In the bowl of a stand mixer fitted with the paddle attachment, combine the cream cheese and sour cream. Beat on medium speed for 3 to 5 minutes, until completely smooth (make sure your cream cheese is at room temperature for the smoothest filling). Add the sugar, salt, vanilla, lemon juice, and lemon zest and mix to combine. Beat in the eggs, one at a time, ensuring each is fully incorporated before adding the next. Scrape down the sides and bottom of the bowl and beat again for 10 seconds. Pour the cheesecake batter into the crust.

Bake for 35 to 40 minutes, until the center just slightly jiggles and the edges are set.

Remove from the oven but keep the oven on. Allow the bars to cool for 10 minutes. Then, in an even layer, spread the sour cream topping over the filling. Return the bars to the oven for 12 minutes. Remove the pan again, turn off the oven, and allow the bars to cool to room temperature. Cover the pan tightly with aluminum foil or plastic wrap and refrigerate the bars for at least 4 hours or overnight.

MAKE THE CHERRY SAUCE

In a small pot, combine the cherries, water, lemon juice, cornstarch, and sugar. Stir together. Cook over medium heat, stirring often, for 5 to 7 minutes, until the mixture bubbles and thickens. Remove from the heat and allow to cool.

SERVE THE CHEESECAKE BARS

Slice the cheesecake into 16 bars, cleaning the knife between cuts with a wet towel, and transfer to individual dessert plates. Spoon the cherry sauce over the bars and serve.

The cheesecake bars, without the sauce, can be stored in the refrigerator, tightly covered, for up to 3 days. Leftover cherry sauce can be kept in a glass container, tightly covered, in the refrigerator for up to 3 days.

Cornbread BLONDIES

MAKES 16 BLONDIES

I didn't know I needed a cornbread blondie in my life until I ordered it from the dessert menu at Inness (a hotel/restaurant/spa complex in upstate New York). Suddenly, I very much needed cornbread blondies in my life quite regularly. It is not a showy dessert. It is exactly as the name states, which is basically a perfectly rendered blondie with a cornbread-like texture. On the savory-sweet spectrum, this is still a sweet dessert with a savory nuance, which lends itself to savory-sweet accompaniments like a drizzle of hot honey. Of course, I am a bit of a purist and would recommend serving with vanilla ice cream (okay, maybe you can drizzle the hot honey on the ice cream). Regardless, accompanied or not, the cornbread blondie is a lovely departure from the regular blondie rotation.

- 6 ounces (12 tablespoons / 170 g) unsalted butter, melted and slightly cooled
- ½ cup (100 g) granulated sugar
- ½ cup firmly packed (110 g) light brown sugar
- ¼ cup (60 ml) honey
- 2 tablespoons full-fat buttermilk
- 1 teaspoon kosher salt
- 1 teaspoon pure vanilla extract
- 1 large egg
- 1 egg yolk
- 1 cup (125 g) all-purpose flour
- 1 cup (160 g) finely ground cornmeal, plus more for topping
- ¼ teaspoon baking soda
- ½ teaspoon baking powder
- Flake sea salt, such as Maldon, for topping (optional, but highly recommended)

Preheat the oven to 350°F (180°C) and position a rack in the center. Butter the sides and bottom of a light-colored metal 8-inch (20-cm) square pan. Line with parchment paper so that it overhangs by about 1 inch (2.5 cm) on two sides of the pan. Butter the paper.

In a large bowl, whisk together the melted butter, granulated and brown sugars, honey, buttermilk, salt, and vanilla. Add the egg and the yolk and whisk to combine. Sprinkle the flour, cornmeal, baking soda, and baking powder over the mixture and, using a spatula, fold the ingredients together until just incorporated. Note: The batter will be super thick.

Transfer the batter into the prepared baking pan and use the flat side of an offset spatula to press into an even layer. Sprinkle the top evenly with a dusting of cornmeal, about 2 teaspoons, and a scattering of flake sea salt, if using.

Bake for 33 to 37 minutes, until the edges are firmly set and the center does not wobble or feel soft to the touch. Remove from the oven, place on a cooling rack, and let the blondies cool completely. Use a small paring knife to release the blondies from the sides of the pan and pull straight up on the parchment to remove them from the pan. Cut and serve.

The blondies will keep in an airtight container at room temperature for up to 3 days.

SURE THING NOTES

Want to lean into the cornbread side of things? Use a medium-grind cornmeal for added texture and crunch.

I was never able to track down the original recipe that inspired mine, but apparently it was a collab between chef Alex Napolitano and pastry chef Maya Gray.

BLACK COCOA BROWNIES

MAKES 16 BROWNIES

The cocoa brownie is a peculiar yet pervasive species of the classic brownie. Like me, you might have first become acquainted with this type of brownie through one of many ubiquitous and inexpensive, yet handy, supermarket baking mixes. The cocoa brownies these mixes produce have a pleasant chewy texture, but they are entirely lacking in flavor. But cocoa brownies deserve a place in your repertoire. When executed correctly, a cocoa brownie is an entirely unique dessert that is also blessedly foolproof. For this recipe, I used the gold standard, Alice Medrich's cocoa brownie recipe, as my jumping-off point and manipulated the ingredients a bit to coax as much flavor potential as possible from these innocuous-looking dark squares. First, you have to add black cocoa. It makes this brownie pop. It not only provides a gorgeous color, but also adds a pleasant bitterness that is reminiscent of high-cacao-content chocolate bars. Second, use a really good grassy or fruity olive oil. Don't worry, the flavor of the olive oil will take a backseat to the cocoa, but it will shine through in degrees and create the perfect fudgy texture. Lastly, this brownie needs a heavy dose of flake sea salt when it comes out of the oven, as a flavor enhancer. The end result: a fudgy, slightly rarefied, slightly adult-tasting confection.

- ¼ cup (20 g) black cocoa powder (see page 26)
- ½ cup (40 g) unsweetened cocoa powder (natural preferred over Dutch-process)
- 2½ ounces (5 tablespoons / 75 g) unsalted butter
- 5 tablespoons (75 ml) extra-virgin olive oil
- 1¼ cups (250 g) granulated sugar
- 2 large eggs
- ½ teaspoon kosher salt
- 1 teaspoon pure vanilla extract
- ½ cup (65 g) all-purpose flour
- 1 generous teaspoon flake sea salt, such as Maldon

Preheat the oven to 325°F (165°C) and position a rack in the center. Butter the sides and bottom of a light-colored metal 8-inch (20-cm) square pan. Line with parchment paper so that it overhangs by about 1 inch (2.5 cm) and butter the parchment.

In a small bowl, whisk together the black and natural cocoa powders and set aside.

Put the butter in a medium bowl and set the bowl in a large skillet filled about halfway to the top with simmering water. Stir the butter until just melted, then add (in this order) the olive oil, sugar, and cocoa powders and stir until just combined. Remove from the heat (you do not want to accidentally burn the cocoa powder). The mixture will be thick and grainy at this point.

Add the eggs, one at a time, and whisk vigorously after each addition until well combined. Whisk in the salt and vanilla. Switch from a whisk to a spatula and add the flour. Fold the flour into the batter until it disappears, then continue to fold for another 30 seconds. Transfer the batter to the prepared pan and smooth the top.

recipe continues next page

Bake for 30 to 40 minutes, until a toothpick inserted into the center of the brownies comes out with a few moist crumbs sticking to it. Remove from the oven and immediately sprinkle with flake sea salt.

Let the brownies cool almost completely (see Sure Thing Note). Use a small paring knife to release the brownies from the sides of the pan and pull straight up on the parchment paper to remove them from the pan. Place on a cutting board, cut into 16 squares, and serve.

Leftover brownies freeze extremely well; just be sure to wrap tightly in plastic wrap or aluminum foil. You can eat the frozen brownies directly from the freezer or allow to thaw for about 30 minutes before serving.

SURE THING NOTE

For a slightly fudgier brownie, you can try this optional step: Before the brownies cool completely, remove them from the pan and wrap them in aluminum foil, then pop them in the freezer. Remove about an hour later and slice them into serving pieces and refreeze and serve frozen as needed. In their frozen state, the brownies take on a melt-in-your-mouth consistency.

MALTED *Crispy Treats*

MAKES 16 BARS

I have been a fan of the ubiquitous crispy treats for ages, and I like them in all their infinite variations. The endless cereal and add-in combos rarely offend and often inspire. For my hot take on this treat, I stayed mostly true to the original formula but erred on the gooier side of things and loaded it up with some malty flavor and bits of whoppers (malted milk balls), which happen to be one of my favorite candies. They are easy and no-bake, and keep well. This is your friendly reminder to make crispy treats more often.

- 3½ ounces (6 tablespoons / 90 g) unsalted butter, cut into ½-inch cubes
- ½ cup (70 g) malted milk powder
- 10 ounces (285 g) mini marshmallows
- 1 tablespoon pure vanilla extract
- ¼ teaspoon kosher salt
- 5 cups (150 g) crispy rice cereal
- 1 cup (135 g) chopped or crushed malted milk balls, plus 6 or 7 malted milk balls, gently crushed, for topping (optional)

Butter the sides and bottom of an 8-inch (20-cm) square baking pan. Line with parchment paper so that it overhangs by about 1 inch (2.5 cm) on two sides of the pan. Butter the paper.

In a medium-size pan, melt the butter over low heat. Once completely melted, whisk in the malted milk powder. It's okay if the powder does not completely melt into the butter, but try your best. With a wooden spoon, stir in the marshmallows until melted. Stir in the vanilla and salt. Remove the pan from the heat and stir in the rice cereal for about 15 seconds before adding the chopped malted milk balls. This will prevent the malted milk balls from melting. Try to ensure the marshmallow mixture coats all of the cereal mixture. Immediately transfer to the prepared pan. Spray the back of a flat metal or silicone spatula and gently press the mixture into an even layer. Try to avoid applying too much pressure. You should be aiming to keep some decent height here.

Sprinkle the gently crushed malted milk balls, if using, over the pan in an even layer and gently press them into the treats. Note: This is purely for visual effect.

Set aside for about 1 hour.

recipe continues next page

SURE THING NOTES

Two quick notes here. One, I highly recommend mini marshmallows. They melt a lot easier and faster than larger ones. You can always slice and dice larger marshmallows, but it is more effort than I want to expend. Two, I generally don't have the patience to slice malted milk balls, so I toss them in a plastic bag, seal it, and gently crush them with a heavy spoon or rolling pin. Ideally you will be left with a mixture of large (for texture) and small chunks.

Use a small paring knife to release the treats from the sides of the pan and pull straight up on the parchment to remove them from the pan. Cut and serve.

Leftovers can be stored tightly covered at room temperature for up to 3 days. If you have to stack the treats, layer with sheets of parchment paper to prevent sticking.

Chewy CARAMEL BLONDIES

MAKES 16 BLONDIES

Blondies are deceptive. In theory, they should be incredibly easy to master, but they are full of pitfalls. I have made many blondies that taste phenomenal the first hour out of the oven, but miraculously—like witchcraft—become drier and more uninteresting seemingly by the minute. I have eaten blondies with the texture of sawdust, and I have seen blondies overcompensate with mounds of chocolate, nuts, and other mix-ins to the point that they are no longer blondies but just an adhesive for other sweets. Thankfully my friend and collaborator, Alex Roberts, devised a blondie that achieves all the things a blondie should be—chewy, with forward molasses flavor, and a texture that is anything but dry. The caramel swirl is a lovely addition and adds even more chewiness, but it is not mandatory.

FOR THE CARAMEL:

½ cup (100 g) granulated sugar

1 tablespoon unsalted butter

¼ cup (60 ml) heavy cream

Pinch kosher salt

FOR THE BLONDIES:

6 ounces (12 tablespoons / 170 g) unsalted butter, melted and slightly cooled

1¼ cups packed (275 g) light brown sugar

¼ cup (50 g) granulated sugar

1 teaspoon kosher salt

1 teaspoon pure vanilla extract

1 large egg

1 egg yolk

1¾ cups (220 g) all-purpose flour

¼ teaspoon baking soda

½ teaspoon baking powder

MAKE THE CARAMEL

In a medium saucepan, cook the granulated sugar over medium-low heat without stirring for 3 to 5 minutes, until the sugar melts and the outer ring begins to brown. Gently tilt the pan from side to side to break up any clumps and continue cooking until the melted sugar is amber brown in color. Add the butter and whisk in the cream and salt, then boil for 1 minute. Set aside to cool until just slightly warm. Note: The caramel sauce needs time to cool and thicken, so prepare it first and let it cool down while mixing the batter.

MAKE THE BLONDIES

Preheat the oven to 350°F (180°C) and position a rack in the center. Butter the sides and bottom of a light-colored metal 8-inch (20-cm) square pan. Line with parchment paper so that it overhangs by about 1 inch (2.5 cm) on two sides of the pan. Butter the paper.

In a large bowl, whisk together the melted butter, brown and granulated sugars, salt, and vanilla. Add the egg and the yolk and whisk to combine. Sprinkle the flour, baking soda, and baking powder over the mixture and, using a spatula, fold the ingredients together until just incorporated. Note: The batter will be super thick.

recipe continues next page

Transfer the batter into the prepared baking pan and use the flat side of the spatula to press into an even layer. Drizzle three or four thick lines of caramel over the batter (use 3 to 4 tablespoons of the caramel and save the rest; see the Sure Thing Note). Use a small knife or toothpick to swirl the caramel into a desired pattern.

Bake for 30 to 33 minutes, until the edges are set. Remove from the oven, place on a cooling rack, and let the blondies cool completely.

Use a small paring knife to release the blondies from the sides of the pan and pull straight up on the parchment to remove them from the pan. Cut and serve.

The blondies will keep in an airtight container at room temperature for up to 3 days.

SURE THING NOTE

The caramel sauce is how we gild the lily. It will add a pleasant, chewy, crackly element to the blondies; but no fear, these blondies can proudly stand on their own. The extra caramel the recipe produces (it is hard to make super small batches of caramel) is quite lovely as an accompaniment to other desserts (brownies, ice cream, and so on . . .). To save the extra caramel, simply pour it into an airtight glass jar once cool and refrigerate for up to 3 weeks. To reheat, place the jar in a small saucepan with warm water until the mixture is fluid, or scoop out into a microwave safe bowl and heat in short bursts until warm and pourable.

NOT YET *Millionaire's* BARS

MAKES 16 BARS

Millionaire's shortbread is the combination of three of my favorite things: buttery shortbread, gooey caramel, and chocolate. Scotland is the birthplace of shortbread, and millionaire's shortbread is just an extension of their famous biscuit. I am a massive fan of the classic recipes, but I also enjoy tinkering. My version, my Not Yet Millionaire's Bars, is similar to the original but different. First, I opted for a salty pretzel crust instead of a shortbread base, because it is slightly faster to make, and I hate burying perfectly good shortbread under so many layers. Second, I made my ganache sliceable. It does not shatter or crack under the blade. The gorgeous caramel layer is unchanged, and when sandwiched between the pretzel crust and ganache top, it gives just enough without squishing out the sides.

FOR THE COCOA PRETZEL CRUST:

- 4 ounces (115 g) salty pretzels
- 3½ ounces (7 tablespoons / 105 g) unsalted butter
- 1 tablespoon unsweetened Dutch-process cocoa powder
- 2 tablespoons light or dark brown sugar

MAKE THE COCOA PRETZEL CRUST

Preheat the oven to 325°F (165°C) and position a rack in the center. Butter the sides and bottom of a light-colored metal 8-inch (20-cm) square pan. Line with parchment paper so that it overhangs by about 1 inch (2.5 cm) on two sides of the pan.

If you have a food processor, pulse the pretzels into chunky crumbs. Be careful not to overprocess into a powder. Alternatively, you can place the pretzels in a plastic bag and crush them with a rolling pin or metal spoon.

In a medium saucepan, gently melt the butter over low heat. Remove from the heat and whisk in the cocoa powder and brown sugar. Stir in the pretzel pieces until combined and turn the mixture into the prepared pan. Use your hands or the back of a measuring cup to press the mixture into the bottom of the pan; do not press it up the sides.

Bake the crust for 10 minutes, then set aside to cool completely.

recipe continues next page

SURE THING NOTE

You do not need a candy thermometer (or instant-read thermometer) to nail the caramel-making portion of this recipe; however, if you have one, please use it. If you do decide to eyeball it, just keep an eye on the color of the condensed milk. Most people tend to pull the caramel too early from the stovetop (still milk-white), but you really want the color of the mixture to be golden, or a light caramel color.

FOR THE CARAMEL LAYER:

- 1 (14-ounce / 400-g) can sweetened condensed milk
- 2 ounces (4 tablespoons / 55 g) unsalted butter
- 2 tablespoons light or dark brown sugar
- 1 tablespoon light corn syrup
- ½ teaspoon kosher salt

FOR THE CHOCOLATE GANACHE LAYER:

- 3 ounces (85 g) dark chocolate, 60 to 75 percent cacao
- ½ teaspoon light corn syrup
- 2 ounces (4 tablespoons / 55 g) unsalted butter
- 1 tablespoon flake sea salt, such as Maldon

MAKE THE CARAMEL LAYER

In a medium saucepan, combine the condensed milk, butter, brown sugar, corn syrup, and salt. Place the saucepan over medium heat and stir the mixture continuously with a heatproof rubber spatula, until the caramel starts to thicken and goes from off-white to golden caramel in color, 10 to 16 minutes. (If you have a candy thermometer, the mixture should read 225°F / 107°C). It is important to continually stir and scrape the bottom of the pan to make sure the caramel does not scorch.

Remove from the heat and pour over the cooled crust. Working quickly, use an offset metal spatula to spread the caramel evenly over the crust. Refrigerate the bars for about 1 hour, or until the caramel layer is cool to the touch.

MAKE THE CHOCOLATE GANACHE LAYER

In a large metal bowl, combine the chocolate, corn syrup, and butter. Set the bowl over a saucepan of simmering water and heat, stirring with a rubber spatula, until the mixture is completely smooth. Remove the bowl from the pan and stir for 30 seconds to cool slightly. Pour the mixture over the chilled caramel layer and use an offset spatula to spread it into an even layer. Sprinkle the flake sea salt over the ganache.

Put in the refrigerator for 1 hour, or until the glaze hardens.

Remove the pan from the refrigerator 30 minutes before serving to prevent cracking of the chocolate glaze. Cut into squares and serve.

The bars can be stored tightly covered in the refrigerator for up to 4 days.

PEANUT BUTTER *Banana* ICEBOX CAKE

MAKES 16 SLICES

Icebox cakes are tailor-made for the warmer months, especially during the long stretches of summer where turning on an oven seems akin to torture. They do require some forward planning, but the forethought is rewarded with silky, smooth, and cool spoonfuls of sweetness. This particular recipe features two of my favorite players: peanut butter and bananas. The peanut butter portion is big, loud, and creamy while bananas mainly take a back seat, as do the wafers. But make no mistake, the simplicity is the selling point. It's a summer crowd pleaser.

- 2 cups (475 ml) heavy whipping cream
- ½ teaspoon pure vanilla extract
- 1½ cups (190 g) confectioners' sugar, divided
- 1 cup (250 g) creamy peanut butter
- 8 ounces (225 g) mascarpone cheese, softened at room temperature
- 1 box Nilla Wafers (11-ounce box)
- 4 large (or 5 medium) ripe bananas, sliced ½ inch (1.3 cm) thick
- ¼ cup (35 g) roasted salted peanuts, chopped, for topping
- 2 tablespoons semi-sweet chocolate chips or cacao nibs for topping

MAKE THE ICEBOX CAKE

You will be using an 8-inch (20-cm) square pan for this recipe. It does not need any prep.

In the bowl of a stand mixer fitted with the whisk attachment, combine the heavy cream, vanilla, and ¾ cup (95 g) of the confectioners' sugar. Whip on medium-high speed until stiff peaks form, 5 to 6 minutes. Scoop out 1 cup (240 ml) of the whipped cream and set aside in the refrigerator to use as the topping for later. Scrape the remainder of the whipped cream into a large bowl.

Wipe down your mixer bowl. Switch to the paddle attachment.

In the bowl of a stand mixer, combine the peanut butter, mascarpone, and the remaining ¾ cup (95 g) of confectioners' sugar. Beat on medium speed until smooth, 1 to 2 minutes. Don't overmix or your mascarpone could become chunky.

Remove the bowl from the mixer and, using a rubber spatula, gently fold the larger quantity of the whipped cream into the peanut butter mixture until smooth and uniform.

recipe continues next page

SURE THING NOTES

I know the freeze-and-thaw step of this cake is not ideal for those in the need of a quick dessert, but it is essential to your icebox texture. Also, I specify the use of Nilla Wafers in this dessert for three reasons. One, they are fairly ubiquitous and easy to find. Two, there is no point in making your own unless you are a masochist: The process is long and the payoff is nil. Three, of course you could sub a chocolate wafer, but I feel like the peanut-forward flavor of this dessert shines with Nilla Wafers and does not need the chocolate accompaniment.

COOKIES

Surprisingly EASY LEMON SHORTBREAD

MAKES 24 COOKIES

There is something uniquely pleasing about a tin full of buttery shortbread on the kitchen counter. The cookies, which seemingly get better a few days after baking them, are somehow more posh than a jar full of chocolate chip cookies and less embarrassingly decadent than a tub full of brownies, but they are equally alluring. These shortbread cookies are also ridiculously easy to make. Simply put all the ingredients into a food processor, dump into a pan, and bake. This specimen of shortbread is crispy but light and full of lemon punch.

- 8 ounces (16 tablespoons / 225 g) cold salted butter, cut into ¼-inch cubes, (see Sure Thing Note on page 93)
- 1 cup (125 g) confectioners' sugar
- 2 cups (250 g) all-purpose flour
- Freshly grated zest of 2 medium lemons
- 1 tablespoon granulated sugar for topping

Preheat the oven to 325°F (165°C) and position a rack in the center. Butter the corners of a light-colored metal 9 by 13-inch (24 by 36-cm) pan. Line the bottom with parchment paper so that it overhangs by about 1 inch (2.5 cm) on two sides of the pan. Butter the paper.

In a food processor, combine the butter, confectioners' sugar, flour, and lemon zest and pulse until the ingredients appear crumbly and sandy. Process for 30 more seconds (or up to 1 minute), until a dough just begins to form. Turn the dough out into the prepared pan, and using your hands or the back of a flat spatula, quickly press it into an even layer. Do not overwork the dough.

Bake for 28 to 30 minutes, until the edges of the shortbread start to turn a very light golden color.

Remove the shortbread from the oven and, using a bench knife or paring knife, cut the dough into eight columns and three rows. Use the tines of a fork to prick each rectangle several times, then sprinkle the granulated sugar over the pan of shortbread. Bake for another 5 to 7 minutes, until the surface of the shortbread is a light golden brown.

Turn off the oven and open the oven door wide to let the heat escape for a few seconds. Place a wooden spoon between the oven door and the oven cavity while the shortbread is still in the oven to help it dry out for an extra crispy shortbread. Remove from the cool oven and make sure the cookies cool completely before breaking them apart.

Shortbread stores beautifully. Just keep it at room temperature in an airtight container for up to 2 weeks.

varations on next page

CACAO *Nib* SHORTBREAD

I love the crunch and visual contrast provided by cacao nibs.

- 1 recipe Surprisingly Easy Lemon Shortbread (page 92)
- 1½ teaspoons pure vanilla extract
- 2 tablespoons cacao nibs

Use the Surprisingly Easy Lemon Shortbread recipe as is except swap the lemon zest for the vanilla extract. Once the dough is formed in the processor, sprinkle the cacao nibs over the top, and pulse for 5 seconds to disperse. Follow the remaining instructions as written.

Holiday SPICE SHORTBREAD

When you need a holiday cookie that keeps extremely well.

- 1 recipe Surprisingly Easy Lemon Shortbread (page 92)
- ⅛ teaspoon ground nutmeg
- ⅛ teaspoon ground cloves
- 1 teaspoon pure vanilla extract
- ½ teaspoon cinnamon

Use the Surprisingly Easy Lemon Shortbread as is except swap the lemon zest for the nutmeg, cloves, and vanilla extract.

Mix the cinnamon with the granulated sugar reserved for topping. Follow the remaining instructions as written.

SURE THING NOTE

To keep the butter cold (which is important here), I suggest cutting the butter into cubes then placing it back in the refrigerator for at least 15 minutes before starting the recipe. Also, no, I do not measure the lemon zest. I literally just toss in the entire zest of two lemons, and it is always just right.

PEANUT BUTTER AND JELLY *Sandwich* COOKIES

MAKES 8 SANDWICH COOKIES

I like to tell people this recipe is inspired by Nutter Butters, the mass-produced peanut butter sandwich cookie made by Nabisco, but that is only a half-truth because I cannot recall the last time I actually ate a Nutter Butter. It's a good reference, nonetheless, because people get very excited about Nutter Butters.

This recipe is not trying to do anything other than be a best-in-class peanut butter cookie with a down-and-dirty buttercream filling, and it overperforms in that respect. It has become a bit of a staple in my house. The cookies are on the softer side, not super crisp, so the filling won't ooze out the sides when biting into the sandwich, and the icing is shot through with peanut butter. It is sweet, but don't fear, it is not too sweet (okay, maybe it is by a tad). You will notice I recommend a jam layer for balance, but truth be told, I make these without the jam just as frequently as I do with the jam. The truly best part of this cookie: It weirdly keeps well in the refrigerator. In theory they should get mushy and wet, but by some strange alchemy the cookies hold up well in the cool environment (covered tightly, of course) and I find myself just eating them directly from the fridge.

FOR THE COOKIES:

- 1¼ cups (155 g) all-purpose flour
- ¾ teaspoon baking soda
- ¼ teaspoon baking powder
- 4 ounces (8 tablespoons / 115 g) unsalted butter, softened
- ½ cup (125 g) peanut butter (Jiff or Skippy works better than all-natural in this recipe)
- ¼ cup (50 g) granulated sugar
- ¾ cup packed (150 g) light brown sugar
- 1 large egg
- 1 teaspoon pure vanilla extract

MAKE THE COOKIES

In a small bowl, whisk together the flour, baking soda, and baking powder.

In the bowl of a stand mixer fitted with the paddle attachment, combine the butter, peanut butter, and granulated and brown sugars. Beat on medium speed until blended. Add the egg and vanilla and mix until the mixture is light and fluffy, about 5 to 6 minutes. Add the flour mixture and mix on low speed until a very soft dough forms. Cover the bowl and refrigerate the dough for at least 3 hours or overnight.

Preheat the oven to 350°F (180°C) and position two racks near the center of the oven. Line two half sheet baking pans with parchment paper.

recipe continues next page

SURE THING NOTE

This dough is super-soft thanks to the inclusion of peanut butter. For the best possible outcome, make sure to chill your dough the required 3 hours, or it will be very tough to portion, and the cookies will spread a lot more. These are perfect to make a day ahead.

FOR THE FILLING:

- 2 ounces (4 tablespoons / 55 g) unsalted butter, softened
- ¼ cup (65 g) peanut butter
- 1½ cups (185 g) confectioners' sugar, divided
- 2 tablespoons whole milk, plus more as needed
- ½ teaspoon pure vanilla extract
- ¼ cup (60 ml) thick berry jam or preserves (Bonne Maman is recommended)

FOR THE ASSEMBLY:

- 1 tablespoon thick berry jam or preserves

Using a medium ice-cream scoop with a release mechanism, form balls of dough (each ball should be about 2 heaping tablespoons / 45 g in size) and place them about 2 inches (5 cm) apart on the prepared baking sheets.

Bake for 13 to 15 minutes, until the cookies start to turn a nut brown (the edges will brown first, but I like to continue baking until the center of the cookies also start to turn golden). Allow the cookies to cool on the pan for a few minutes before transferring them to a wire rack to cool completely.

MAKE THE FILLING

In the bowl of a stand mixer fitted with the paddle attachment, beat the butter and peanut butter on medium speed until smooth and creamy, 2 to 3 minutes. Add half of the confectioners' sugar and beat on low speed for 1 minute. Add about 90 percent of the remaining confectioners' sugar and beat for another minute. Add the 2 tablespoons of milk, then add the vanilla and jam and mix on high speed until light and fluffy. The buttercream should be stiff. If the buttercream seems too loose, add the remaining confectioners' sugar, 1 tablespoon at a time, until you get the correct consistency. Alternatively, if the filling appears too thick, add more milk in 1-teaspoon increments until it loosens up enough to sandwich.

ASSEMBLE THE SANDWICH COOKIES

Match up the cookies in pairs for sandwiching. Smear a thin layer of jam on one cookie and spread (or plop) a generous scoop of the peanut butter filling on the opposite cookie. Literally sandwich them together, gently pressing until the filling spreads to the edge of the cookie. Repeat until all of the cookies are complete. Place the cookies on a plate or small tray, cover, and refrigerate for 30 minutes to firm up before serving.

Store the cookies in an airtight container in the refrigerator for up to 3 days. Alternatively, the cookies will keep at room temperature (in an airtight container), but the filling may become soft.

PEANUT BUTTER M&M COOKIES

The peanut butter cookies in the peanut butter sandwich cookie recipe are delightful as is. They make a respectable peanut butter cookie on their own, or you can dress them up with a handful of regular M&Ms.

Follow the cookie recipe exactly and fold in ¾ cup (150 g) M&Ms after the flour addition, but before you chill them. Makes 16 cookies.

Peanut Butter–Filled CHOCOLATE THUMBPRINT COOKIES

MAKES 20 COOKIES

For me, these are holiday-time cookies and they are not in my regular all-year rotation. They are delicious and delightful, but sometimes I just can't be bothered with the filling and topping components and will gravitate toward my most basic cookie recipes (see page 43 for Choose Your Own Adventure Chocolate Chip Cookies). Or, somewhat shamefully, I will make the cookie base and just dollop Nutella into the thumbprint (see variation on opposite page). That said, I have to remark that these are exceptional cookies when made as directed. The base is crispy and crunchy, and the filling is an all-American peanut butter burst. Finally, the dark chocolate drizzle adds both a welcome contrast to the nutty sweet filling as well as some visual appeal, and the whole thing is worthy of a holiday soiree or special event.

FOR THE THUMBPRINT COOKIES:

1 cup (125 g) all-purpose flour

¼ cup (25 g) unsweetened Dutch-process cocoa powder

¼ teaspoon kosher salt

4 ounces (8 tablespoons / 115 g) unsalted butter, softened

½ cup (100 g) granulated sugar

1 large egg yolk

1 teaspoon pure vanilla extract

MAKE THE THUMBPRINT COOKIES

In a small bowl, whisk together the flour, cocoa powder, and salt.

In the bowl of a stand mixer fitted with the paddle attachment, beat the butter and sugar together at medium-high speed until smooth and creamy. Scrape down the sides and bottom of the bowl, add the egg yolk and vanilla and beat until the mixture is light and fluffy, about 5 to 6 minutes. Add the flour mixture and mix on low speed until a very soft dough forms. Cover the bowl and chill the dough for about 15 minutes. This should make it easier to make the "thumbprint."

Line two half sheet baking pans with parchment paper.

Using a small ice-cream scoop with a release mechanism, form balls of dough (each ball should be about 2 heaping teaspoons / 25 g in size) and place them about 1½ inches (4 cm) apart on the prepared baking sheets. If the dough still feels too soft, return it to the refrigerator to firm up.

SURE THING NOTE

While these are called thumbprint cookies, more often than not, I use a dowel or the backside of a teaspoon to make the imprint so the well is more even and deep and consistent. Thumbs work, but the wells will most likely look a bit erratic.

FOR THE PEANUT BUTTER FILLING:

¼ cup plus 2 tablespoons (100 g) creamy peanut butter

3 tablespoons confectioners' sugar, sifted

½ teaspoon pure vanilla extract

FOR THE CHOCOLATE DRIZZLE TOPPING:

2 ounces dark chocolate, 60 to 75 percent cacao, coarsely chopped

Flake sea salt, such as Maldon, to finish

Use a very clean finger, thumb, or the dowel tip side of a wooden spoon to create a ½-teaspoon indentation in the center of each cookie, pressing down gently. Be careful not to go all the way through the cookie, and make sure to widen the indentation so that it can hold a lot of filling.

Place the baking sheets with the cookie dough in the refrigerator to rest for 30 to 45 minutes to help the cookies hold their shape during baking.

Preheat the oven to 350°F (180°C) and position two racks near the center of the oven.

Bake the cookies for 8 to 10 minutes, or until the edges are set, though the inner walls of the cookie might look a bit soft. If you are baking both sheet pans at once, be sure rotate from top to bottom halfway through the baking time to ensure consistency. Remove the cookies from the oven and use the back of a teaspoon (in place of your thumb) to reinforce the indentation. Cool completely while you make the filling.

MAKE THE PEANUT BUTTER FILLING

In a small bowl, use a rubber spatula to vigorously stir together the peanut butter, confectioners' sugar, and vanilla until smooth. If the filling feels overly firm, pop it into the microwave for 10 seconds to loosen it up. Scrape the filling into a piping bag and fill the completely cooled cookies with the peanut butter filling.

MAKE THE CHOCOLATE DRIZZLE TOPPING

Melt the chocolate in a double boiler or in the microwave (see page 33 for both methods).

Use another small piping bag to crisscross each cookie with thick chocolate lines. Or, if you want to skip the whole pastry bag thing (like me), just dip the tines of a large fork into the chocolate and wave it over the cookies (it is a messier look but the end product is equally delicious). Sprinkle the tops of the cookies with flake sea salt.

Chill the cookies in the refrigerator for about 15 minutes before serving.

The cookies can be stored in an airtight container at room temperature for up to 3 days. I tend to keep the cookies covered tightly in the refrigerator because I prefer the firmer texture they take on in the refrigerator.

Nutella-Filled THUMBPRINT COOKIES

This variation uses Nutella in place of the peanut butter filling. Warm up ½ cup (120 ml) of Nutella in a microwave before adding it to a piping bag. Fill the thumbprint cookies with Nutella and top with toasted hazelnuts. I have also been known to pipe warmed-up jarred cookie butter directly into the indentations and sprinkle the cookies with cinnamon.

CRISPY, *Chewy*, UGLY, THIN, *Delicious* CHOCOLATE CHIP COOKIES

MAKES 20 COOKIES

I bake often. And when prepping a cookbook or testing a bunch of recipes, I tend to bake a lot more than often. It was during one of these whirlwind recipe development stages that this cookie was born. I was in the process of remaking one of my latest chocolate chip cookie recipes (of which I have too many) and I somehow put the dry flour mix from another recipe I was working on simultaneously (not a good idea) in the cookie dough. I should have known immediately. The dough looked odd, almost soupy, but I chilled it, scooped eight dough balls, and popped them in the oven. What came out of the oven was a super-thin, amorphous layer of crispy cookies all melding into each other. Normally, I would toss a kitchen disaster directly in the garbage. I don't like wasting extra calories on half-assed cookies. But I took a nibble. Then another. Then I broke it up into cookie shards and ate the rest throughout the week. This recipe is a less untidy version of what came out of my oven. The edges are super crispy and buttery, and they give in the middle to a bit of molasses-tinged chew. It is a more alien, but equally desirable, version of my favorite chocolate chip cookie.

- 8 ounces (16 tablespoons / 225 g) unsalted butter
- 1½ cups (190 g) all-purpose flour
- 1 teaspoon baking soda
- 1 teaspoon kosher salt
- 1 cup (200 g) granulated sugar
- ¾ cup packed (165 g) light brown sugar
- 2 large eggs
- 1 tablespoon pure vanilla extract
- 10 ounces (280 g) semisweet chocolate chips

Melt the butter in a microwave or over low heat in a saucepan until just melted, not browned.

In a large bowl, whisk together the flour, baking soda, and salt. Set aside.

In a separate large mixing bowl, combine the granulated and brown sugars and pour in the melted butter. Whisk the mixture vigorously until smooth. Add the eggs, one at a time, and whisk until combined. Whisk in the vanilla.

Pour the dry ingredients into the egg mixture and use a spatula to bring the mixture together—almost as if you were folding in dry ingredients for a cake batter. Once the mixture is mostly uniform, stir in the chocolate chips. The dough will look less firm than a traditional cookie dough. Cover the bowl and place in the refrigerator for at least an hour or up to overnight.

recipe continues next page

Preheat the oven to 350°F (180°C) and line two half sheet baking pans with parchment paper. While the oven heats, use a medium ice-cream scoop with a release mechanism (or a small spoon and your hands) to form balls of 2 to 3 heaping tablespoons (25 to 40 g) and place on the prepared cookie sheet 3 to 4 inches (7.5 to 10 cm) apart. These cookies spread out.

Bake for 11 to 13 minutes, until the edges of the cookies are medium brown and the very middle is still a bit pale. Feel free to cool the cookies directly on the pan before serving, but obviously feel free to serve them slightly warm.

The cookies can be stored in an airtight container at room temperature for up to 3 days.

SURE THING NOTES

A few things to keep in mind here before you go rogue (that is, adapt this recipe to your liking). One, you have to use chocolate chips (mini chocolate chips are even better), not chocolate chunks. The cookie is too thin to support chunky chocolate. Two, oven temp really matters here. Make sure the oven is at temperature before you start baking. Three, I have baked these directly after mixing and after refrigerating for an hour or so, and I think I prefer the refrigerated dough by a hair.

MOLASSES *Ginger* COOKIES

MAKES 24 TO 30 COOKIES, DEPENDING ON THE SCOOP SIZE

Initially, I was trying to find a way to get all cute with the traditional molasses ginger cookie by adding nontraditional ingredients or updating time-tested ratios, but this was an idea I quickly quashed. A good ginger molasses cookie doesn't really need an update. This is a fairly standard—and absolutely delicious—take on the classic. And feel free to play with the bake time. I tend to prefer baking these cookies on the longer side of the bake time for a bit more texture.

- 3¼ cups (405 g) all-purpose flour
- 2 teaspoons ground ginger
- 1 teaspoon ground cinnamon
- ½ teaspoon ground cloves
- ½ teaspoon ground nutmeg
- ¼ teaspoon ground cardamom
- ¼ teaspoon instant espresso powder
- ½ teaspoon baking soda
- ¼ teaspoon kosher salt
- 1⅓ cups (265 g) granulated sugar, divided
- ½ cup packed (110 g) dark brown sugar
- 2 tablespoons freshly grated ginger (see Sure Thing Note)
- 8 ounces (16 tablespoons / 225 g) unsalted butter, softened, cut into ½-inch cubes
- 6 tablespoons (90 ml) unsulfured molasses
- 1 large egg
- 1 teaspoon pure vanilla extract

In a medium bowl, whisk together the flour, ginger, cinnamon, cloves, nutmeg, cardamom, espresso powder, baking soda, and salt. Set aside.

In the bowl of a stand mixer fitted with the paddle attachment, beat together 1 cup (200 g) of the granulated sugar, the brown sugar, and freshly grated ginger on medium speed until well combined, about 1 minute. Add the butter and beat the mixture on medium speed until light and fluffy, about 3 minutes. Add the molasses, egg, and vanilla. Beat until thoroughly combined. Add about half of the dry ingredient mixture to the butter mixture and mix on low speed until almost combined. Add the remaining dry ingredients and mix until just combined. Do not overmix. Scrape dough into a bowl, cover with plastic wrap, and referigerate for 1 hour.

Preheat the oven to 350°F (180°C), positioning the racks in the middle. Line two half sheet baking pans with parchment paper. Place the remaining ⅓ cup (65 g) of the granulated sugar in a wide rimmed bowl.

While your oven heats up, use a medium ice-cream scoop with a release mechanism (or a small spoon and your hands) to form balls of 1½ to 2 heaping tablespoons (15 to 25 g). Roll the cookies through the sugar to coat completely and place on the prepared cookie sheets about 2 inches (5 cm) apart.

Bake for 12 to 13 minutes, until the edges are set and you see a few cracks form on top. If you are baking both sheet pans at once, be sure rotate from top to bottom halfway through the baking time to ensure consistency. Remove from the oven and allow the cookies to cool on the baking sheets for a few minutes before transferring them to a wire rack to cool completely.

The cookies can be stored in an airtight container for up to 3 days.

SURE THING NOTE

I realize that fresh ginger is not something you might have lying around your kitchen. If you happen to have some, it adds a lovely bit of character to these cookies. Simply use a microplane to grate the required amount. If you do not have fresh ginger, you can, and still should, make these cookies. Just amp up the ground ginger (by 1 to 2 extra teaspoons) when blending the dry ingredients.

CHOCOLATE RYE COOKIES

MAKES 10 COOKIES

Why rye? True, rye is not a ubiquitous flour lurking in everyone's cupboard, but I did notice (however anecdotally) that it is becoming a bit more common due to the increasing popularity of homemade sourdough. In short, the addition of rye flour here adds a hint of nuttiness and complements the cocoa and chocolate beautifully. These cookies hit the chocolate craving hard. It's a simple cookie to make with a surprisingly complex flavor. My friends describe this cookie as "less sweet" than most and "brownie-like." I describe them as "perfect" and "worthy" of any cookie plate.

⅔ cup (85g) all-purpose flour

½ cup (60g) rye flour

⅓ cup (35g) dark cocoa powder

½ teaspoon baking soda

½ teaspoon kosher salt

1 teaspoon espresso powder

4 ounces (8 tablespoons / 115 g) unsalted butter, softened, cut into 1-inch cubes

⅔ cup (133g) granulated sugar

¼ cup (50g) brown sugar

½ teaspoon pure vanilla extract

1 large egg

½ cup (90g) dark chocolate chunks, about 60 to 70 percent cacao

Fleur de sel, for sprinkling

In a large bowl, whisk together the flour, rye flour, cocoa powder, baking soda, salt, and espresso powder.

In the bowl of a stand mixer fitted with the paddle attachment, beat the butter, granulated and brown sugars, and vanilla on medium speed until light and fluffy, about 3 minutes. Add the egg and beat until smooth. Add the dry ingredients all at once and mix on the lowest setting until no dry streaks remain. Lastly, add the chocolate chunks and mix in until distributed evenly. Cover the bowl with plastic wrap or a large plate and refrigerate for 10 to 15 minutes.

Preheat the oven to 350°F (180°C) and line a half sheet baking pan with parchment paper.

Using a small ice-cream scoop with a release mechanism (or a small spoon and your hands), form dough balls—about 2½ tablespoons (2 ounces / 55 grams)—and place them about 2 inches apart on the prepared baking sheet. Sprinkle the top of each cookie with a little fleur de sel.

Bake 12 to 14 minutes, until slightly puffed and cracking. Note: It is harder to tell when a chocolate-colored cookie is done (you won't have any telltale signs of browning), so I advise to always err on the side of pulling these cookies near the earlier suggested bake time (gooier is better than dry). Bang the pan on the counter right before letting the cookies cool. Allow the cookies to cool directly on the baking sheet for a few minutes before serving.

The cookies can be stored in an airtight container for up to 3 days.

SURE THING NOTE

If you don't have rye flour on hand, feel free to swap out the rye for another low-gluten flour (or, in a pinch, use general all-purpose flour) in a one-to-one ratio. It's worth noting that buckwheat flour is a great alternative to rye here because it's gluten-free and has a similar nutty flavor. You can use any cocoa powder you like here, but I love the way a dark (or super "Dutched") cocoa like Valrhona's gives these cookies an aesthetically pleasing dark and moody appearance.

RED *Velvet* COOKIES

MAKES 18 TO 24 COOKIES

For a brief moment in time, red velvet cake swept the nation. It was a dessert trend that proved to have longer legs than some of its peers. But, as with all high-velocity fad cycles, interest in it eventually peaked and slowly faded away to the back of the bakery case. This is a shame. Red velvet cake, essentially a buttermilk cocoa cake covered in cream cheese frosting, is a notable dessert. This recipe is merely an homage to this once famous cake. It is not meant to be the cake in cookie form. Instead, this cookie is a fun adaptation with the texture of a classic chocolate chip and deep cocoa flavor cut through with some chunky milk chocolate. I love interspersing these cookies on a tray of blonde and chocolate ones. The red really pops!

- 1½ cups (190 g) all-purpose flour
- ¼ cup (20 g) unsweetened Dutch-process cocoa powder
- ½ teaspoon baking soda
- ¼ teaspoon kosher salt
- 4 ounces (8 tablespoons / 115 g) unsalted butter, softened
- ¼ cup packed (55 g) light brown sugar
- ¾ cup (150 g) granulated sugar
- 1 large egg, at room temperature
- 2 teaspoons pure vanilla extract
- 1½ teaspoons red gel food coloring
- 1 teaspoon white vinegar
- 1 cup (170 g) milk chocolate chunks
- ¼ cup (50g) granulated sugar for rolling

In a medium bowl, whisk the flour, cocoa powder, baking soda, and salt together. Set aside.

In the bowl of a stand mixer fitted with the paddle attachment, beat the butter, brown sugar, and ¾ cup (150 g) of the granulated sugar on medium speed until light and creamy, about 3 minutes. Scrape down the sides and bottom of the bowl and add the egg, vanilla, and 1 tablespoon of water. Beat on medium speed for about 1 minute, until combined. Add the food coloring and mix until the batter is uniform in color.

Add the dry ingredients and turn the mixer on low speed to stir until the batter forms a very soft dough. Add the vinegar and chocolate chunks and beat again on very low speed until the chunks are dispersed evenly. Cover the mixing bowl with plastic wrap and refrigerate for about 2 hours.

Preheat the oven to 350°F (180°C) and position the oven racks in the middle. Line two half sheet baking pans with parchment paper. Put the remaining ¼ cup (50 g) granulated sugar in a shallow bowl.

While your oven heats up, use a medium ice-cream scoop with a release mechanism (or a small spoon and your hands) to form balls (of 1½ to 2 heaping tablespoons). Roll the cookies through the granulated sugar to coat completely and place on the prepared cookie sheets about 2 inches (5 cm) apart.

recipe continues next page

Bake for 11 to 13 minutes, until the edges appear set. If you are baking both sheet pans at once, be sure rotate from top to bottom halfway through the baking time to ensure consistency. Usually, at the 10-minute mark I use a "bang the pan" technique (see Sure Thing Note).

Remove from the oven and allow the cookies to cool on the baking sheets for a few minutes before transferring them to a wire rack to cool completely.

The cookies can be stored in an airtight container for up to 3 days.

SURE THING NOTE

Ever since I baked Sarah Kieffer's incredibly delicious and popular Pan-Banging Chocolate Chip Cookies (from her cookbook *Vanilla Bean Baking*), I literally bang the pan on all cookie recipes to test it out (Sarah writes extensively about which batters work best for this on her website, The Vanilla Bean Blog). Turns out that these cookies do have a little more personality if you bang the pan toward the end of the bake time. At the 10-minute mark, when the cookies are a bit puffy in the center, pick up the pan while in the oven and drop it on the oven rack and continue to bake until finished.

SOFT AND FROSTED SUGAR COOKIES *(à la Lofthouse cookie)*

MAKES 24 COOKIES

Somehow, until fairly recently, I was unaware of Lofthouse sugar cookies. It was only after they entered my social media algorithm that I was even aware this was a style of cookie. Perhaps because I spent a very long time confined to New York City and Lofthouse sugar cookies are associated with traditional grocery stores and New York City real estate is not welcoming to traditional grocery stores (though that is slowly changing)? Whatever the reason, I am glad I found them later in life. As mentioned, these cookies are ubiquitous in grocery stores throughout North America thanks to Lofthouse Foods, and the texture is a cakey, crumbly sugar cookie dolled up with heaps of frosting and sprinkles. They are addictive and light in the way that shortbread is, but they are much cuter.

FOR THE COOKIES:

2½ cups (310 g) all-purpose flour
¼ cup (30 g) cornstarch
1 teaspoon baking powder
½ teaspoon baking soda
½ teaspoon kosher salt
4 ounces (8 tablespoons / 115 g) unsalted butter, softened
1 cup (200 g) granulated sugar
2 large eggs
1 teaspoon pure vanilla extract
½ cup (120 g) sour cream

MAKE THE COOKIES

In a medium bowl, whisk together the flour, cornstarch, baking powder, baking soda, and salt. Set aside.

In the bowl of a stand mixer fitted with the paddle attachment, cream together the softened butter and granulated sugar until light and fluffy, 2 to 3 minutes.

Add the eggs, one at a time, beating well after each addition.

Add the vanilla extract and half of the flour mixture to the creamed butter mixture. Turn the mixer to the lowest setting and beat on low for 20 to 30 seconds. Add the sour cream all at once and beat for another 20 to 30 seconds. Scrape the bottom and sides of the bowl and add the remaining flour mixture and stir (again, on the lowest setting) until just combined. Do not overmix.

Line two half sheet baking pans with parchment paper. Using a small ice-cream scoop with a release mechanism, form balls of dough (approximately 2 heaping tablespoons / 40 g in size) and place them about 2 inches (5 cm) apart on the prepared baking sheets. (Refer to Sure Thing Note for scooping suggestion). If you can fit them, place the pans in the refrigerator for 45 minutes. If the pans don't fit in your refrigerator, you

recipe continues next page

FOR THE FROSTING:

4 ounces (8 tablespoons / 115 g) unsalted butter, softened

3½ cups (440 g) confectioners' sugar, plus more if needed

¼ cup (60 ml) heavy cream, plus more if needed

1 teaspoon pure vanilla extract

⅛ teaspoon fine sea salt

Food coloring (optional)

Sprinkles (optional)

may have to place the dough balls side-by-side into a smaller container and then place them on the baking sheet after they have been refrigerated. Cover the mixing bowl with plastic wrap or a plate and chill the dough for at least 30 minutes or up to 2 hours to make them easier to portion.

Preheat the oven to 350°F (180°C) and position two racks near the center of the oven.

Bring the pans out of the refrigerator and use the palm of your hand to gently flatten the dough balls a tiny bit (until they are about ¼ inch / 6 mm thick). Use a light touch; you are not trying to mash them into flat pancakes.

Bake for 10 to 12 minutes, until the edges are just beginning to turn golden. Note: I really think these taste best the exact minute before they start to turn golden, so make sure to remove them from the oven the minute they start to take on a hint of color.

Allow the cookies to cool on the baking sheets for a few minutes before transferring them to wire racks to cool completely.

MAKE THE FROSTING

In the bowl of a stand mixer fitted with the paddle attachment, cream the softened butter until smooth and creamy.

Gradually add the confectioners' sugar, 1 cup (125 g) at a time, mixing well after each addition.

Add the heavy cream, vanilla, and salt. Beat on medium-high speed until the frosting is smooth and fluffy. If you'd like to add food coloring, do so at this point and mix until the desired color is achieved. The frosting should be thick but spreadable. If the frosting feels too thick, add more heavy cream, 1 tablespoon at a time, until you reach the desired consistency. On the other hand, if the frosting feels too loose, add more confectioners' sugar, 1 tablespoon at a time, until you think it is spreadable, yet thick enough to hold its shape.

ASSEMBLE

Once the cookies are completely cool, spread a generous amount of frosting onto each cookie. Decorate with sprinkles, if using. Allow the frosting to set before serving. Cookies can be stored tightly covered at room temperature for up to 3 days.

SURE THING NOTE

People go to great lengths to make these cookies perfectly round, but in the interest of time and sanity, I just recommend you portion the cookies with an ice-cream scoop. Dip the scoop in hot water every few cookies, and you should have mostly exquisite circular cookies with—at most—a tiny bit of variation.

BLACK SESAME *White Chocolate* COOKIES

MAKES 12 COOKIES

I had to include this cookie in the book. I am aware that it might be a bit out of the Sure Thing category in that it includes atypical ingredients and a few more steps than usual, but it is a personal favorite of mine and means a great deal to me. I stumbled upon a variation of this cookie at Hart Bageri in Copenhagen and fell so deeply for it that it was all I thought about for days after returning home. This is not their recipe. I never contacted the bakery (maybe I should have) for specifics, but this recipe is an attempt to bring the essence of my time in Copenhagen home via a very unusual, but highly enjoyable cookie.

- 1½ cups (190 g) all-purpose flour
- ½ teaspoon baking soda
- ½ teaspoon kosher salt
- 4 ounces (8 tablespoons / 115 g) unsalted butter, softened
- ⅔ cup (135 g) granulated sugar
- ½ cup packed (110 g) light brown sugar
- 3 large egg yolks
- 2 tablespoons black sesame paste or black tahini
- ½ teaspoon pure vanilla extract
- 1 cup (170 g) white chocolate chips
- 3 tablespoons black sesame seeds for rolling
- 1 tablespoon flake sea salt, such as Maldon (optional)

In a medium bowl, whisk together the flour, baking soda, and salt. Set aside.

In the bowl of a stand mixer fitted with the paddle attachment, beat the butter and granulated and brown sugars on medium speed until light and fluffy, about 3 minutes. Scrape down the sides and bottom of the bowl. Add the egg yolks, black sesame paste, and vanilla. Beat on medium speed for about 1 minute, or until combined.

Add the dry ingredients and beat on the lowest setting until the batter forms a very soft dough. Add the white chocolate chips and beat again on the lowest speed until the chips are dispersed evenly. Cover the mixing bowl with plastic wrap and refrigerate for about 15 minutes (or while your oven heats up).

Preheat the oven to 350°F (180°C), positioning the racks in the middle. Line two half sheet baking pans with parchment paper. Add the black sesame seeds to a small bowl.

recipe continues next page

SURE THING NOTE

Black sesame paste comes in many forms and with many names. While I typically can find this ingredient at my local Asian market, you can also easily find it online. It comes in large plastic pouches and small, medium, and large jars. It is also sold as black tahini. Just note that, like an all-natural peanut butter, you will likely have to stir or massage the oily bits into the thicker paste until the consistency is uniform before using.

While your oven is heating up, remove the bowl from the refrigerator and use a medium ice-cream scoop with a release mechanism (or a small spoon and your hands) to form balls of about 2 tablespoons. Run the dough balls through the black sesame seeds to coat and place them about 2 inches (5 cm) apart on the prepared baking sheets. Using the palm of your hand, gently press down on each dough ball (do not try to flatten too much). Sprinkle the top of each cookie with a little flake sea salt, if using.

Bake for 13 to 14 minutes, until the edges appear set. If you are baking both sheet pans at once, be sure to rotate from top to bottom halfway through the baking time to ensure consistency.

Remove from the oven, and bang/drop the cookie sheet once or twice against the counter to help them spread a tiny bit more. Let the cookies cool on the baking sheet for a few minutes before transferring them to a wire rack to cool completely.

The cookies can be stored in an airtight container at room temperature for up to 3 days.

Pumpkin WHOOPIE PIES REDUX

MAKES 10 WHOOPIE PIES

The original version of this recipe appeared in my first baking book (co-authored by Renato Poliafito), *Baked: New Frontiers in Baking*. The recipe was a smash hit, and it was circulated widely and evidently made frequently. I feel compelled to include the updated version of this recipe, because it is indeed a Sure Thing. It is a recipe that is easy to make, and it is well worth the minor effort. Not only are whoopie pies visually pleasing, but these pumpkin whoopies are perfect. The cakes are slightly dense but still moist and spiced with hints of fall. They are filled and held together with the sweet tang of cream cheese frosting. I made a few changes to the original: halved the recipe (you can easily double this), made the spices more balanced, and got rid of some of the fussiness around the cream cheese filling. It's still one of my favorite recipes.

FOR THE COOKIES:

1½ cups (190 g) all-purpose flour

½ teaspoon kosher salt

½ teaspoon baking powder

½ teaspoon baking soda

1 tablespoon ground cinnamon

1½ teaspoons ground ginger

½ teaspoon ground cloves

¼ teaspoon ground nutmeg

½ cup (120 ml) vegetable oil

1½ cups (360 g) pumpkin puree, chilled

1 large egg

1 teaspoon pure vanilla extract

1 cup packed (220 g) dark brown sugar

MAKE THE COOKIES

Preheat the oven to 350°F (180°C), positioning the racks in the middle, and line two half sheet baking pans with parchment paper and set aside.

In a large bowl, whisk together the flour, salt, baking powder, baking soda, cinnamon, ginger, cloves, and nutmeg. Set aside.

In another large bowl, whisk together the oil, pumpkin puree, egg, and vanilla until well combined. Add the brown sugar and whisk until combined.

Sprinkle the flour mixture over the pumpkin mixture and whisk until fully incorporated.

Use a small ice-cream scoop with a release mechanism to form the whoopie cookies, roughly 2 heaping tablespoons in size. Drop onto the prepared baking sheets, about 1 inch (2.5 cm) apart.

Bake for about 15 minutes, until the cookies are just starting to crack on top and a toothpick inserted into the center of one cookie comes out clean. Let cool completely on the pans.

recipe continues next page

FOR THE CREAM CHEESE FILLING:

2 ounces (4 tablespoons / 55 g) unsalted butter, softened

4 ounces (115 g) cream cheese, room temperature

1½ cups (190 g) confectioners' sugar

1 teaspoon pure vanilla extract

MAKE THE CREAM CHEESE FILLING

In the bowl of a stand mixer fitted with the paddle attachment, beat the butter on medium speed until smooth. Add the cream cheese and beat until well combined and lump-free. Add the confectioners' sugar and vanilla and beat just until smooth.

ASSEMBLE THE WHOOPIE PIES

Line a half sheet baking pan with parchment paper and turn over half the whoopie pies so that the flat side is facing up. When the cookies have cooled completely, use a medium ice-cream scoop with a release mechanism to scoop and release the filling on the flat side of half of the cookies. Sandwich with the remaining cookies, pressing down slightly so that the filling spreads to the edge of the cookies. Cover the baking sheet with plastic wrap. Refrigerate the whoopie pies for at least 30 minutes (or overnight) before serving.

The whoopie pies can be kept tightly covered in the refrigerator for up to 3 days.

SURE THING NOTE

I generally use the same size ice-cream scoop for the cookie and the filling—it works beautifully. But you can also just use a large spoon or, if you want a slightly nicer finish, feel free to pipe the filling directly onto the cookie. Trust me, there is no wrong way.

MY FAVORITE HOLIDAY COOKIES
(That I Make All Year Long)

It would be a disservice to both the Peanut Butter Blossom and the Chocolate Crinkle Cookie to file them away as only "holiday" or "Christmas" cookies because they really deserve to be made all year long.

PEANUT BUTTER *Blossom*

MAKES 36-48 COOKIES

This was, hands down, my favorite cookie growing up. I asked my mom to make many of them for every holiday, but also every birthday and special occasion that called for cookies (bake sales, teacher appreciation day, sleepovers). The cookie is both an ode to all peanut butter cookies, and to Hershey's oddest confection, the Hershey's Kiss.

I just always assumed that the Peanut Butter Blossom was created by Hershey's to help sell more Hershey's Kisses, but the original recipe is credited to Freda Smith, who entered this cookie in the 1957 Pillsbury Bake-Off contest. The cookie didn't win the bake-off (some horrible-looking confection called Accordion Treats did), but it found everlasting fame in the years that followed. This version of the Peanut Butter Blossom hues somewhat closely to the original, as there is no need to rework a masterpiece.

SURE THING NOTE

Many recipes will suggest you avoid "all-natural" peanut butter in Peanut Butter Blossoms to help hold their shape, but I generally only have the all-natural stuff on hand, and it works just fine. If you are using all-natural, like me, be sure to stir all the oil back into the peanut butter so it is mixed thoroughly and chill the dough for an extra 15 to 30 minutes before scooping and baking.

36 to 48 Hershey's Kisses (original milk chocolate)

1½ cups (170 g) all-purpose flour

1 teaspoon baking soda

½ teaspoon kosher salt

¼ cup (50 g) vegetable shortening

2 ounces (4 tablespoons / 55 g) unsalted butter, cool but not cold

¾ cup (195 g) creamy peanut butter

⅓ cup (65 g) granulated sugar

⅓ cup firmly packed (75 g) dark brown sugar

1 large egg

2 tablespoons whole milk

1 teaspoon pure vanilla extract

⅓ cup demerara sugar

Remove the wrappers from all the Hershey's Kisses and place the chocolates in a bowl. Set aside.

In a medium bowl, whisk together the flour, baking soda, and salt.

In the bowl of a stand mixer fitted with the paddle attachment, beat the shortening and butter on medium-high speed until smooth. Add the peanut butter and beat again on medium speed until combined, about 1 minute. Scrape down the sides and bottom of the bowl and add both the granulated and brown sugars. Beat on medium speed until the mixture is fluffy, about 2 minutes. Add the egg, milk, and vanilla and beat until completely blended, 1 to 2 minutes. Scrape down the sides and bottom of the bowl and add the flour mixture all at once. Beat on low-medium speed until completely incorporated, about 1 minute.

Cover the bowl with plastic wrap, and place in the fridge while your oven preheats.

Preheat the oven to 375°F (190°C). Line two half sheet baking pans with parchment paper. Place the demrara sugar in a small, shallow bowl.

When your oven comes to temperature, remove the bowl from the refrigerator and use a medium ice-cream scoop with a release mechanism (or a small spoon and your hands) to form balls of about 1½ tablespoons. Run the dough balls through the demerara sugar to coat and place them on the prepared baking sheets about 2 inches (5 cm) apart. Bake until the cookies appear dry to the touch, about 8 to 10 minutes.

Remove the sheets from the oven and place on cooling racks. Immediately, gently press a Hershey's Kiss into the center of each cookie, making sure it's good and snug so it doesn't fall out when cooled. The cookie will crack around the edges. Cool completely and serve.

The cookies can be kept tightly covered at room temperature for up to 3 days.

THE CHOCOLATE *Crinkle*

MAKES 30 COOKIES

The chocolate crinkle cookie is having a mini resurgence. Once relegated primarily to holidays, no doubt due to its "snow-like" confectioners' sugar exterior, the crinkle is starting to pop up on year-round bakery menus and evolving beyond its chocolate origins. I have recently seen "crinkles" in lemon, red velvet, and even ginger varieties.

A good crinkle cookie is light in texture, nearly melt-in-your-mouth. It is also important to drench—not dust—them in confectioners' sugar so the visual contrasting pop of the chocolate cracks and white sugar is punched up to eleven. My recipe is quite literally adapted from my mom's recipe that was most likely scrawled out from one of her ladies' magazines of yore. I pushed the chocolate flavor hard here and even suggest you sprinkle with fleur de sel (mainly because I would sprinkle fleur de sel on everything).

- 1¼ cups (160 g) all-purpose flour
- 2 tablespoons unsweetened Dutch-process cocoa powder
- ½ teaspoon baking powder
- ¼ teaspoon kosher salt
- 6 ounces (170 g) dark chocolate (60 to 70 percent cacao), coarsely chopped
- 2 ounces (4 tablespoons / 55 g) unsalted butter, cut into ½-inch cubes
- 2 large eggs, room temperature
- ¼ cup (50 g) granulated sugar
- ½ cup firmly packed (110 g) light brown sugar
- 2 teaspoons pure vanilla extract
- ¾ cup (85 g) confectioners' sugar
- 2 tablespoons fleur de sel (optional)

In a medium bowl, whisk together the flour, cocoa powder, baking powder, and salt.

Melt the chocolate and butter together using the microwave or double-boiler method (see page 33). Stir occasionally, until the chocolate and butter are completely melted, smooth and combined. Remove from the heat and cool to room temperature.

In the bowl of a stand mixer fitted with the paddle attachment, beat the eggs and both the granulated and brown sugars on medium speed until smooth, about 3 to 4 minutes. Add the vanilla and scrape in the chocolate mixture. Beat on medium speed until combined, about 2 minutes. Scrape down the sides and bottom of the bowl and add the flour mixture all at once. On the lowest possible speed, beat the mixture until just incorporated. Do not overmix. Cover the bowl tightly and refrigerate the dough for at least 2 hours and up to 24 hours.

SURE THING NOTE

This is already a very chocolate-y cookie. However, if you want to enhance the chocolate flavor even more, stir a teaspoon of espresso powder into the melted chocolate. You won't really taste the espresso flavor, but it does add a certain depth that will mostly be appreciated.

Preheat the oven to 350°F (180°C) and line two half sheet baking pans with parchment paper. Place the confectioners' sugar in a small, wide bowl.

Remove the dough from the refrigerator and use a medium ice-cream scoop with a release mechanism (or a small spoon and your hands) to form balls (each about 2 heaping tablespoons). Roll them in confectioners' sugar to coat—you really want these covered in the sugar, so it almost looks like a snowball without a lot of chocolate showing through—and place them on the prepared baking sheets about 1½ inches (4 cm) apart.

Bake the cookies until they start to firm up around the edges, about 9 to 12 minutes. If you want a gooier center, remove on the earlier side.

Remove the sheet pans from the oven and while the cookies are still warm, sprinkle them with the (optional) fleur de sel. Transfer the cookies to a cooling rack to cool completely before serving.

The cookies can be kept tightly covered at room temperature for up to 2 days.

CIAMBELLINE *al Vino Rosso* (ITALIAN RED WINE COOKIES)

MAKES 24 COOKIES

On a recent trip to Rome, I signed up a small group of friends for a food tour winding its way through the Mercato Trionfale, an enormous, modern, covered market near the Vatican. Obviously, the market is astounding. It is overflowing with fresh pastas and produce and olive oils and perfect specimens of meat and fish, but it was the ciambelline al vino rosso that we remember most. It is the cookie we (okay, my friend Roger Braimon) still talk about. These Italian red wine cookies are crunchy and flavorful without being too sweet. The cinnamon-sugar coating gives it texture and zing. I believe these cookies are traditionally served after a meal with red wine, but they are divine with espresso and coffee as well. Roger was able to track down the recipe from the stall that sold him his favorite batch (I believe it came from Mani Pasta Pasta), and they shared their recipe, which I adapted here.

FOR THE CINNAMON-SUGAR TOPPING:

- 2 tablespoons granulated sugar
- ½ teaspoon ground cinnamon

FOR THE RED WINE COOKIES:

- ½ cup (100 g) granulated sugar
- ½ teaspoon baking powder
- ½ teaspoon kosher salt
- 2 cups (250 g) all-purpose flour
- 7 tablespoons (100 ml) Lambrusco or any red wine
- 7 tablespoons (100 ml) extra-virgin olive oil
- 1 teaspoon sambuca liqueur (optional)

MAKE THE CINNAMON-SUGAR TOPPING

In a shallow bowl, stir together the sugar and cinnamon. Set aside.

MAKE THE RED WINE COOKIES

Preheat the oven to 350°F (180°C) and line two half sheet baking pans with parchment paper.

In a large mixing bowl, whisk together the sugar, baking powder, salt, and flour. Make a well in the center and add the wine, olive oil, and liqueur, if using. Use a wooden spoon to combine until a shaggy dough forms. Turn the dough out onto a work surface and knead with your hands until the dough feels uniform, about 30 seconds.

recipe continues next page

SURE THING NOTES

Give yourself some grace during the shaping process and don't become too fixated on making each "rope" the exact same length and width. I just plop a school ruler on my counter as a way to eyeball the length as I go, but each one ends up slightly different. Also, the cinnamon topping is divisive. Some folks think the cinnamon overpowers the red wine flavor too much. I suggest you do a taste test by making some with a cinnamon-sugar and some just with sugar before making any hard decisions.

Pinch off about 1 heaping tablespoon of dough and roll it out into a rope 5 to 6 inches (13 to 15 cm) in length and about ½ inch (1.3 cm) in width (it does not have to be exact). Shape into circles with the ends overlapping by about ½ inch (1.3 cm). Pinch gently to seal the ends.

Dip the top half of your biscuits in the cinnamon-sugar mixture to coat and then place them on the prepared baking sheet—sugar side facing up—about ½ inch (1.3 cm) apart.

Bake for 31 to 35 minutes, until nice and golden. (Note: Thicker ropes will take slightly longer to bake.) Remove from the oven and allow to cool completely on the pans.

Store the cookies in an airtight container at room temperature for up to a week.

Oatmeal Cream SANDWICH COOKIES

MAKES 12 COOKIES

This recipe is another throwback. It is a direct tribute to the cellophane-wrapped, industrially made oatmeal cream pies that were the best part of my school lunchbox. In this homemade homage, I made the "pies" more cookie-like—crispier—while still full of old-fashioned oats. I also added a pinch of fall flavors, and I sized them appropriately. When you sandwich the tangy cream cheese filling between each bite-size cookie, you are making the perfect "right from the refrigerator" snack.

FOR THE OATMEAL COOKIES:

1 cup (125 g) all-purpose flour
1 cup (90 g) old-fashioned rolled oats
1 teaspoon ground cinnamon
½ teaspoon ground ginger
⅛ teaspoon ground nutmeg
½ teaspoon baking powder
¼ teaspoon baking soda
¼ teaspoon kosher salt
4 ounces (8 tablespoons / 115 g) unsalted butter, softened
¼ cup (50 g) granulated sugar
¼ cup packed (55 g) light brown sugar
1 tablespoon unsulfured molasses
1 large egg

MAKE THE OATMEAL COOKIES

In a medium bowl, whisk together the flour, oats, cinnamon, ginger, nutmeg, baking powder, baking soda, and salt in a small bowl. Set aside.

In the bowl of a stand mixer fitted with the paddle attachment, beat the butter, the granulated and brown sugars, and the molasses on medium speed until light and fluffy, 2 to 3 minutes. Add the egg and beat until smooth.

Add the dry ingredients all at once and mix on the lowest setting until a dough forms. Remove the bowl from the mixer, cover with plastic wrap, and chill in the refrigerator for 1 hour.

Preheat the oven to 350°F (180°C), positioning the racks in the middle, and line two half sheet baking pans with parchment.

Using a small ice-cream scoop with a release mechanism or a small spoon and your hands, form about 1 tablespoon of the dough into balls of about ¾ ounce (20 g). Place them 2 inches (5 cm) apart on the prepared baking sheets. If the dough feels warm from being handled, refrigerate the dough balls directly on the baking pans for about 15 minutes before placing in the oven.

Bake on the middle rack for 8 to 10 minutes, until the cookies have spread and turned a light golden brown on the edges.

Allow the cookies to cool completely directly on the baking sheets.

recipe continues next page

SURE THING NOTE

The filling on this cookie is decidedly soft on purpose for both texture and taste purposes. However, you can always thicken the cream cheese filling by adding an extra ½ cup (25 g) of confectioners' sugar if you prefer a stiffer filling that will give less "squish" with each bite.

FOR THE FILLING:

2 tablespoons unsalted butter, softened

4 ounces (115 g) cream cheese, at room temperature

2¾ cups (345 g) confectioners' sugar

1 teaspoon pure vanilla extract

MAKE THE FILLING

In the bowl of a stand mixer fitted with the paddle attachment, beat the butter and cream cheese on medium speed until smooth and lump free. Add the confectioners' sugar and vanilla and beat until just incorporated and the filling is smooth. The filling will be loose before refrigerating. Refrigerate the bowl for 15 minutes.

ASSEMBLE THE OATMEAL CREAM SANDWICH COOKIES

Line a half sheet baking pan with parchment paper and turn over half the cookies so that the flat side is facing up. When the cookies have cooled completely, spoon or pipe 2 to 3 tablespoons of filling on the flat side of the upturned cookies. Ever so gently sandwich with the remaining cookies by pressing down slightly so that the filling spreads to the edge of the cookies. Cover the pan with plastic wrap. Refrigerate the cookies for 30 to 60 minutes before serving.

Store the cookies tightly covered in the refrigerator for up to 3 days.

OATMEAL COOKIES WITH *Chocolate Chips*

There are very few cookies that don't benefit from a handful of chocolate chips. You don't actually need them, but there is absolutely no reason not to add them for that retro lunchbox vibe.

Follow the recipe on page 125 to make the oatmeal cookie dough. Stir in 6 ounces (170 g) of semisweet chocolate chips after the dough forms but before you chill it. Instead of scooping mini cookies, I usually use my regular classic cookie scoop (closer to 2 tablespoons) for these. Makes 12 medium-size cookies or 24 small cookies, depending on the scoop size.

SHEET, STACKED, AND LOAF STYLE

EASY DONUT CAKE (WITH *Two Different* TOPPINGS)

SERVES 12

The entire concept for this cake was to emulate the look of a giant frosted donut. The thought process: Donuts are fun. Big donuts are more fun. The cake is a classic anywhere, anytime Bundt with a faint old-fashioned flavor thanks to the addition of the nutmeg. The crumb is tender and light and holds up well under a thick donut glaze that must (well, not really) be covered in a smattering of sprinkles.

FOR THE CAKE:

3½ cups (440 g) all-purpose flour

½ teaspoon ground nutmeg

¼ teaspoon ground cinnamon

¾ teaspoon kosher salt

1 teaspoon baking powder

¼ teaspoon baking soda

10 ounces (20 tablespoons / 275 g) unsalted butter, softened

¼ cup (60 ml) vegetable oil (or another neutral oil like sunflower oil or canola oil)

2 cups (400 g) granulated sugar

½ cup packed (110 g) light brown sugar

1 tablespoon pure vanilla extract

4 large eggs, at room temperature

1 cup (240 ml) full-fat buttermilk

MAKE THE CAKE

Preheat the oven to 350°F (180°C) and position a rack in the lower third of the oven (not the very bottom). Butter and flour a 10 to 12-cup (2.4 to 2.8-L) Bundt pan so that flour covers most of the pan. (See page 31 for how to prepare a Bundt pan.)

In a large bowl, whisk together the flour, nutmeg, cinnamon, salt, baking powder, and baking soda. Set aside.

In the bowl of a stand mixer fitted with the paddle attachment, cream together the butter, oil, granulated and brown sugars, and vanilla on medium speed until light and fluffy, about 3 minutes. Add the eggs one at a time, beating well after each addition. Scrape down the sides of the bowl with a spatula to ensure even mixing.

Add the flour mixture and the buttermilk in two additions, beating on medium speed between each addition until just incorporated. Scrape the bottom of the bowl and mix again for 30 seconds. Scrape the batter into the prepared pan.

Bake for 55 to 65 minutes, until a toothpick inserted in the center of the cake comes out clean. The cake will be deep golden brown.

Remove the pan from the oven and let cool for 20 minutes (set a timer!). Before releasing the cake, tap the bottom of the pan on the counter a few times and lightly bang a butter knife around the sides to help release. Then, carefully invert the cake onto a wire rack and remove the pan. Allow the cake to cool completely with the decorative side up.

recipe continues next page

TOPPING OPTION ONE FOR THE GLAZE:

- 1½ cups (190 g) confectioners' sugar, plus more as needed
- 2 tablespoons whole milk
- ¼ teaspoon pure vanilla extract
- Pinch kosher salt
- Rainbow sprinkles, for topping

TOPPING OPTION TWO FOR THE CINNAMON-SUGAR TOPPING:

- ½ cup (105 g) demerara sugar
- 1 tablespoon ground cinnamon
- 2 ounces (4 tablespoons / 55 g) unsalted butter, melted

MAKE THE GLAZE

In a small bowl, whisk together the confectioners' sugar, milk, vanilla, and salt. The glaze should be thick and ropy, but pourable—not runny and thin. If the glaze looks too thin, add confectioners' sugar, one tablespoon at a time, until you get the desired thickness.

Pour the glaze over the crown of the cake in thick ribbons; it will slowly drip down the sides. Let set for about 15 minutes before serving.

The cake will keep in an airtight container at room temperature for up to 3 days.

OR MAKE THE CINNAMON-SUGAR TOPPING

In a small bowl, stir together the demerara sugar and cinnamon.

Brush the melted butter over the crown of the Bundt cake, then sprinkle with the cinnamon-sugar mixture. Let set for about 5 minutes before serving.

The cake will keep in an airtight container at room temperature for up to 3 days.

SURE THING NOTES

You could probably lose the nutmeg and cinnamon (however heartbreaking this would be to me) if those spices don't do a lot for you, and it would still be a great cake. However, I would then punch up the vanilla—double it even—and maybe zest something citrusy into the cake batter for something a bit more unique. Also, I provided two different toppings so you can make either one (I do not recommend both) depending on the dessert mood you are in.

EASY SUMMER STRAWBERRY CAKE

SERVES 10 TO 14

This is a summer cake. It is casual enough to make for an outdoor barbeque, but it is also boho-chic and elegant, and it would even shine bright in a more formal twilight-dinner-under-the-stars affair. Most importantly, for a two-layer cake, it is quite easy to make and assemble, yet it is still impossibly addictive. It is the kind of cake you will crave all summer long. The flavorful cake layers are hearty with a nod to pound cake (another favorite summer dessert), and the buttercream is silky and lush with the perfect hint of strawberry. Overall, it is neither too sweet nor too heavy, so feel free to reach for a second slice.

FOR THE CAKE:

- 2¼ cups (280 g) all-purpose flour
- 1½ teaspoons baking powder
- ½ teaspoon kosher salt
- 6 large eggs, at room temperature
- 1½ cups (300 g) granulated sugar
- 6 tablespoons (90 ml) neutral oil, such as vegetable or canola
- ⅓ cup (80 ml) whole milk, at room temperature
- 1½ teaspoons pure vanilla extract

MAKE THE CAKE

Preheat the oven to 350°F (180°C) and position a rack in the center. Butter the sides and bottom of two 9-inch (23-cm) round cake pans. Line the bottoms with parchment paper and butter the paper.

In a medium bowl, whisk together the flour, baking powder, and salt. Set aside.

In the bowl of a stand mixer fitted with the whisk attachment, whip the eggs and sugar on low speed to combine, then increase the speed to medium-high and whip for 3 to 5 minutes, until the mixture turns pale yellow and fluffy. While the mixer is still running, slowly pour in the oil until combined. Remove the bowl from the mixer.

Pour half of the flour mixture into the egg mixture and fold in slowly with a rubber spatula for a minute or two. The mixture should not be fully combined at this point. Add the milk and vanilla and stir again for another minute before adding the remaining flour mixture. Continue to fold the mixture just until a smooth batter forms. Divide the batter evenly between the two pans and smooth the tops.

Bake for 20 to 24 minutes, until the tops are just starting to turn golden brown and the cakes spring back from the center when gently pressed. Alternatively, you can check for doneness by sticking a toothpick into the center of the cakes. The cakes are done if the toothpick comes out clean. Check early and often so you don't overbake them.

recipe continues next page

FOR THE STRAWBERRY BUTTERCREAM:

6 large strawberries, diced, plus a handful of fresh strawberries for decorating

¼ cup (50 g) granulated sugar

2 ounces (4 tablespoons / 55 g) unsalted butter, softened

1 (8-ounce / 225-g) container mascarpone cheese or cream cheese, at room temperature

4½ cups (560 g) confectioners' sugar, plus more as needed

1 teaspoon pure vanilla extract

FOR THE ASSEMBLY:

½ cup (120 ml) strawberry preserves or jam

Invert the cakes onto a cooling rack, remove the pans, remove the parchment, and invert the cakes again so the tops are facing upwards. Let cool completely while you make the buttercream.

MAKE THE STRAWBERRY BUTTERCREAM (SEE SURE THING NOTE BELOW)

In a small saucepan over medium heat, stir together the diced strawberries and granulated sugar. Cook the mixture for 4 to 5 minutes, or until bubbling and thickened. Use an immersion blender (or blender) to blend until smooth. Alternatively, use a fork or potato masher (not ideal, but one less appliance) to mash into a puree.

In the bowl of a stand mixer fitted with the paddle attachment, beat the butter and mascarpone or cream cheese on medium speed until very smooth and creamy, 2 to 3 minutes. Add the confectioners' sugar, vanilla, and 3 tablespoons of the cooled strawberry puree (or 3 tablespoons of strawberry jam or preserves) and beat until combined. If the frosting seems too loose, add additional confectioners' sugar, 1 tablespoon at a time, until it becomes thicker.

TO ASSEMBLE

Place one cooled cake layer on a serving platter. If necessary, trim the top to create a flat surface. Spread ¼ cup of the strawberry preserves in an even layer across the cake. Spoon just under half the buttercream on top of the preserves and spread into an even layer. Add the top cake layer. Spread the remaining ¼ cup of preserves on top, followed by the remaining buttercream. This is a casual cake, and I leave it a bit naked, with exposed sides, but you should have enough buttercream if you want to coat and cover the entire cake. Decorate with sliced, halved, or whole strawberries. Once finished, chill the cake in the refrigerator before slicing and serving.

This cake will keep beautifully in a cake saver in the refrigerator for up to 3 days.

SURE THING NOTES

Want to make this recipe even easier and faster? Simply skip making the puree from scratch and sub in 3 heaping tablespoons of your favorite strawberry jam. Also, if you prefer a tangier frosting or if you can't be bothered looking for mascarpone cheese, you can swap the mascarpone for cream cheese in a one-for-one substitution.

Coconut SHEET CAKE

SERVES 12 TO 16

In my personal dessert hierarchy, coconut cake has never been at the top of my pyramid, but I have always appreciated it. After many years of living in the South, I have fond memories of big, buoyant Southern-style coconut cakes: embarrassingly thick layers and even thicker swathes of filling and frosting, topped and dusted in a nest of coconut shreds. I also have a few friends who prize coconut flavors. This cake is for them. It is created as a sheet cake that leverages my current favorite ratio of thin cake and icing layers, but it is also more casual and easier to assemble than your typical layer cake, and it is bursting with coconut flavor. It is the kind of cake you don't need a special occasion for. You only need a few friends who love coconut.

FOR THE CAKE:

- 2 cups (230 g) all-purpose flour
- 1 teaspoon baking powder
- ½ teaspoon baking soda
- ½ teaspoon kosher salt
- 2 large eggs, separated
- ¼ teaspoon cream of tartar
- 2 tablespoons plus ⅔ cup (25 g plus 135 g) granulated sugar
- 4 ounces (8 tablespoons / 115 g) unsalted butter, softened
- ¼ cup (60 ml) coconut oil
- 1 teaspoon pure vanilla extract
- 1½ teaspoons coconut extract (optional)
- ⅔ cup (160 ml) canned coconut milk, at room temperature
- ⅔ cup (60 g) shredded sweetened coconut

MAKE THE CAKE

Preheat the oven to 350°F (180°C) and position a rack in the center. Butter the sides and bottom of a light-colored metal 9 by 13-inch (24 by 36-cm) pan. Line with parchment paper so that it overhangs by about 1 inch (2.5 cm) on two sides of the pan. Butter the paper.

In a medium bowl, whisk together the flour, baking powder, baking soda, and salt. Set aside.

In a bowl of a stand mixer fitted with the whisk attachment, whip the egg whites on medium-high speed until they look foamy. Right before soft peaks start to form (about 4 to 6 minutes), stop the mixer and add the cream of tartar. Turn the mixer back to medium speed and stream in the 2 tablespoons of sugar. Turn up the speed to high and keep whipping until stiff peaks form. Scrape the mixture into a small bowl and set aside.

Wipe down your mixing bowl. Switch to the paddle attachment.

In the bowl of your stand mixer, combine the butter, coconut oil, remaining ⅔ cup sugar, vanilla, and coconut extract, if using. Beat on medium speed until light and fluffy, 1 to 2 minutes. Add the egg yolks and beat to combine.

recipe continues next page

FOR THE WHIPPED CREAM CHEESE FROSTING:

6 ounces (170 g) cream cheese, at room temperature

1 cup (240 ml) heavy cream

1 cup (125 g) confectioners' sugar

1 teaspoon pure vanilla extract

Shredded coconut for topping (optional)

Add half of the flour mixture. Turn the mixer to the lowest setting and beat for 20 to 30 seconds. Add the coconut milk all at once and beat for another 20 to 30 seconds. Scrape the bottom and sides of the bowl and add the remaining flour mixture and beat (again, on the lowest setting) until just combined. The batter might look chunky at first, but it will smooth out.

Remove the bowl from the mixer. Using a rubber spatula, gently fold in half the whipped egg whites in two additions. Finally, stir in the shredded coconut.

Scrape the batter into the prepared pan and smooth out the top.

Bake for 22 to 24 minutes, until a toothpick inserted in the center of the cake comes out clean. Remove from the oven, place on a cooling rack, and let the cake cool completely.

To remove from the pan, use a small paring knife to release the cake from the sides of the pan and pull straight up on the parchment paper. Place the cake on a large serving platter.

MAKE THE WHIPPED CREAM CHEESE FROSTING

In the bowl of a stand mixer fitted with the paddle attachment, beat the cream cheese on high speed until it is smooth and ribbony, 1 to 2 minutes. Turn the mixer to low-medium speed and stream in the heavy cream. Stop the mixer, scrape down the bowl, and mix on high speed for 1 to 2 minutes, until the mixture is fluffy. Add the confectioners' sugar and vanilla and mix until combined.

Frost the cake. Top with more shredded coconut, if using. Chill for 30 minutes before serving.

The cake will keep tightly covered in the refrigerator for up to 3 days. Slice and serve while cool or at room temperature.

SURE THING NOTES

Two quick things: One, coconut milk has a tendency to separate, so make sure to whisk the liquid and fat together before measuring. Two, I marked the coconut extract as optional in the ingredient list, but it does add a boldness of flavor if you are looking for more coconut punch.

AFTER-DINNER CHOCOLATE CAKE WITH *Mint Ganache*

SERVES 10 TO 14

A good portion of this book is dedicated to informal recipes because I tend to bake casually much more often than not. However, I wanted to include a handful of recipes that wouldn't look out of place in a slightly more formal setting, and this After-Dinner Chocolate Cake with Mint Ganache is a truly gorgeous centerpiece. The cake itself is rich, but not cloying, and it is oh-so-moist because it is oil-based instead of butter-based, which means you don't have to turn to an electric mixer for help. The frosting is a bit of a throwback. It's a delightful and easy-to-manage confectioners' sugar affair, but it is always a crowd-pleaser. Of course, it is the ganache—a velvety, minty ganache—that slightly elevates the experience. The overall effect is an elegant after-dinner mint in the form of a cake. Serve with red wine or cold milk. Either option works amazingly well.

FOR THE CHOCOLATE CAKE:

- 1½ cups (195 g) all-purpose flour
- 1 teaspoon kosher salt
- 1 teaspoon baking soda
- ½ teaspoon baking powder
- ⅔ cup (78 g) unsweetened Dutch-process cocoa powder
- ⅔ cup hot water
- 1⅓ cups (265 g) granulated sugar
- ½ cup (120 ml) vegetable oil (or another neutral oil like sunflower or canola oil)
- 2 large eggs
- ½ cup (120 ml) full-fat buttermilk
- 1 teaspoon pure vanilla extract

MAKE THE CHOCOLATE CAKE

Preheat the oven to 350°F (180°C) and position a rack in the center. Butter the sides and bottom of two 9-inch (23-cm) round cake pans and line the bottoms with parchment paper. Butter the paper.

In a medium bowl, whisk together the flour, salt, baking soda, and baking powder. Set aside.

In a large bowl, whisk together the cocoa powder and hot water until the cocoa powder is dissolved. Add the sugar, oil, eggs, buttermilk, and vanilla and very gently whisk until combined. Sprinkle the dry ingredients over the wet ingredients and whisk until combined. Divide the batter evenly between the two pans and lightly tap the pans on the counter to even out the batter if needed.

Bake for 18 to 22 minutes (check early and often so you don't overbake the cakes), until a toothpick inserted into the center of the cake comes out with moist crumbs. Invert the cakes onto a cooling rack, remove the pans, remove the parchment, and invert the cakes again so the tops are facing upward. Let cool completely.

recipe continues next page

FOR THE BUTTERCREAM FROSTING:

6 ounces (12 tablespoons / 170 g) unsalted butter, softened

2½ cups (300 g) confectioners' sugar, plus more if needed

½ cup (50 g) unsweetened cocoa powder

3 tablespoons heavy cream, plus more if needed

½ teaspoon pure vanilla extract

Pinch kosher salt

FOR THE GANACHE:

8 ounces (225 g) dark chocolate chips or coarsely chopped dark chocolate, 60 to 75 percent cacao

1¼ cups (300 ml) heavy cream

1¼ teaspoon mint extract

MAKE THE BUTTERCREAM FROSTING

In the bowl of a stand mixer fitted with the paddle attachment, beat the butter on medium speed until very smooth and creamy, 2 to 3 minutes. Add the confectioners' sugar, cocoa powder, heavy cream, and vanilla and beat on low speed until almost combined. Increase the speed to medium-high and beat until fluffy, 1 to 2 minutes. If the frosting seems too loose, add additional confectioners' sugar, 1 tablespoon at a time, until it becomes thicker. Alternatively, if the frosting appears too thick, add heavy cream in 1 teaspoon increments, until it loosens up enough to spread and hold.

ASSEMBLE

Place one cooled cake layer on a serving platter. If necessary, trim the top to create a flat surface. Spoon just under half the buttercream on top of the cake and spread into an even layer. Add the top cake layer. Spread the remaining buttercream, coating to cover the entire cake, even if it is a very thin layer. Ideally you want the top and sides to be flat. Once finished, chill the cake in the refrigerator for 30 minutes. At the 30-minute mark, go ahead and start preparing the ganache.

MAKE THE GANACHE

Put the chocolate in a medium-size heatproof bowl and set aside.

In a small saucepan over low heat, whisk together the heavy cream and mint extract. Bring the mixture to a gentle simmer (tiny bubbles will form around the edges of the pan; it should not be a rolling boil). Remove from the heat and pour over the dark chocolate. Let the mixture sit for about 3 minutes. Starting in the center of the bowl, and working your way out to the edges, whisk the chocolate ganache until smooth.

Let the mixture sit for about 10 minutes. The ganache should be almost at room temperature at this point. Remove the cake from the refrigerator and slowly pour the ganache onto the center of the cake. It will spread out to the edge and drip down the sides. Once you have achieved your desired drip-look, place the cake back in the refrigerator for another 30 minutes to set before slicing.

This cake will keep beautifully in a cake saver in the refrigerator for up to 3 days.

SURE THING NOTE

Yes, for the mint adverse, you can skip the mint, but I beg you to try it as is first. The mint itself is purposefully only in the ganache so as not to overpower. I am not a massive mint lover myself, but I love the way it interacts with this cake. If you still have concerns, just cut back on the extract a bit before completely eliminating it.

UPSTATE PUMPKIN BUNDT CAKE *with Maple Syrup Glaze*

SERVES 12 TO 16

I tend to Bundt a lot. If you need a cake to look attractive or elegant, and you don't feel like fussing with layers and filling and frosting and oh-so-perfect finishing, I highly suggest you get Bundt-y as well. Unlike the picnic-style, one-layer snack cakes, Bundts offer a height and preciseness that could suffice as both centerpiece and social media darling. This pumpkin cake is a lightly spiced fall beauty. It is lighter than a traditional pumpkin cake—not weighed down by oil—and it hits all the right notes for a fall weekend upstate—or anywhere that puts you in a fall leaf-peeping, apple-picking, bonfire-building state of mind. Oh, and I offer this cake to you with two toppings to choose from. Both are delicious, but my friends tend to prefer the maple syrup glaze.

FOR THE PUMPKIN BUNDT CAKE:

2½ cups (300 g) all-purpose flour

2 teaspoons baking powder

1 teaspoon baking soda

½ teaspoon kosher salt

1 teaspoon ground cinnamon

1 teaspoon pumpkin-pie spice

¼ teaspoon ground cardamom

Pinch finely ground black pepper

1 cup (220 g) canned pumpkin puree

½ cup (120 g) sour cream

½ cup (120 ml) pumpkin beer

1 teaspoon pure vanilla extract

4 ounces (8 tablespoons / 115 g) unsalted butter, softened

1½ cups (300 g) granulated sugar

3 large eggs

MAKE THE PUMPKIN BUNDT CAKE

Preheat the oven to 350°F (180°C) and position a rack in the center. Grease and flour a 10 to 12-cup (2.4 to 2.8-L) Bundt pan, ensuring you coat the entire surface. (See page 31 for how to prepare a Bundt pan.)

In a medium bowl, whisk together the flour, baking powder, baking soda, salt, cinnamon, pumpkin-pie spice, cardamom, and black pepper. Set aside.

In a separate bowl, whisk together the pumpkin puree, sour cream, beer, and vanilla until smooth. Set aside.

In the bowl of a stand mixer fitted with the paddle attachment, beat the butter and sugar on medium speed until light and fluffy, about 4 to 6 minutes.

Add the eggs, one at a time, beating well after each addition. Pour in the pumpkin puree mixture and beat until smooth and well combined. Add the flour mixture all at once and beat at the lowest setting just until the flour is incorporated. Do not overbeat. Pour the batter into the prepared Bundt pan and smooth the top. Tap the pan gently on the counter to remove any air bubbles.

recipe continues next page

FOR THE MAPLE SUGAR TOPPING (OPTION ONE):

¼ cup (50 g) granulated sugar

¼ cup (35 g) maple sugar

1 teaspoon ground cinnamon

3 ounces (6 tablespoons / 90 g) unsalted butter, melted

FOR THE MAPLE SYRUP GLAZE (OPTION TWO):

1½ ounces (3 tablespoons / 45 g) unsalted butter, melted

5 tablespoons (75 ml) real maple syrup, at room temperature

½ teaspoon ground cinnamon

2 tablespoons heavy cream, plus more if needed, at room temperature

1½ cups (190 g) confectioners' sugar, plus more if needed

Bake for 40 to 50 minutes, until a toothpick inserted into the center of the cake comes out clean. In order to make sure the cake does not overbake, check the cake at 40 minutes and every 3 to 5 minutes thereafter.

Let the cake cool in the pan for about 15 minutes. Then, carefully invert the cake onto a wire rack, remove the pan, and allow it to cool completely with the decorative side up. Place the cooling rack over a sheet pan. This will help to catch excess sugar (for easier cleanup) in the next step.

MAKE THE MAPLE SUGAR TOPPING

Stir together the granulated sugar, maple sugar (see Sure Thing Note below), and cinnamon. Brush the top and sides of the cake with the melted butter and immediately sprinkle with the sugar mixture. You might have to use your hands to press the sugar onto the cake to adhere.

MAKE THE MAPLE SYRUP GLAZE

Whisk together the melted butter, maple syrup, cinnamon, heavy cream, and confectioners' sugar. The glaze should be thick and ropy, but pourable—not runny and thin. If glaze looks too thin, add confectioners' sugar, 1 tablespoon at a time, and whisk to combine. If glaze looks too thick, add heavy cream, ½ teaspoon at a time, to thin it out.

Pour the glaze over the room-temperature cake in thick ribbons; it will slowly drip down the sides. Let set for about 15 minutes before serving.

The cake will keep in an airtight container at room temperature for up to 3 days.

SURE THING NOTES

There are some slightly not-pantry-staple ingredients listed here, so let me offer my substitutions. If you don't feel like foraging for pumpkin beer, you can just use a dark ale in its place. Pumpkin-pie spice is essentially just a mix of cinnamon, clove, nutmeg, and ginger, so you can just substitute ¼ teaspoon of each. And finally, I don't advocate searching high and low for maple sugar (for the sugar topping). You can simply substitute it one-for-one with regular or coarse sugar and increase the cinnamon to 2 teaspoons.

HOHO CAKE
(*Swiss Roll Chocolate Cake*)

SERVES 16

My affinity for Swiss roll–style cakes most likely can be attributed to my fondness for the mass-market Hostess HoHos that I devoured during my grade school years. HoHos, essentially a mini version of a vanilla-filled chocolate sponge Swiss roll covered in an industrial version of ganache, were everywhere in my formative years in Florida. Growing up, I thrived on many shelf-stable packaged baked goods like Twinkies, Entenmann's Donuts, and Little Debbie cakes. But it was the HoHo that became my most consistent object of affection. This recipe is one giant, much-better-tasting, HoHo.

Like all Swiss rolls, it takes a tiny bit of practice and patience to roll the cake without cracking it. However, even if you do break the cake during the roll, all evidence can be covered up with the chocolate ganache shell. Obviously, it is delicious—a chocolate powerhouse with three contrasting components—but it is also fun to serve big pinwheel slices of cake.

FOR THE CAKE:

- ½ cup (65 g) all-purpose flour
- ⅓ cup (30 g) unsweetened Dutch-process cocoa powder
- 1 teaspoon baking powder
- ½ teaspoon kosher salt
- 4 large eggs, separated
- ¾ cup (150 g) granulated sugar, divided
- 1 teaspoon pure vanilla extract
- 2 tablespoons vegetable oil (or another neutral oil like canola or sunflower oil)
- 2 tablespoons confectioners' sugar

MAKE THE CAKE

Preheat the oven to 350°F (180°C) and position a rack in the center. Coat a 10 by 15-inch (25 by 38-cm) jelly roll pan with nonstick baking spray and line it with parchment paper. Lightly spray the paper with nonstick baking spray.

In a small bowl, whisk together the flour, cocoa powder, baking powder, and salt. Set aside.

Combine the egg whites and ¼ cup (50 g) of the granulated sugar in the bowl of a stand mixer fitted with the whisk attachment. Beat on medium-high speed until medium peaks form, about 1 to 3 minutes. Transfer the egg white mixture to a small bowl and set aside.

Wipe down the mixing bowl and swap the whisk for the paddle attachment. Add the egg yolks, vanilla, and the remaining ½ cup of granulated sugar (100 g). Beat on high speed until the mixture is very thick and pale yellow, about 4 to 6 minutes. Add the oil and beat on medium speed until combined. Add the flour mixture and mix on low-medium speed to combine.

recipe continues next page

FOR THE FILLING:

1¼ cups (300 ml) heavy cream

½ cup (65 g) confectioners' sugar

1 tablespoon pure vanilla extract or vanilla paste

Using a rubber spatula, gently fold the beaten egg whites into the yolk mixture in three additions. At first, the mixture will be thick and slightly hard to fold, but it will loosen up as you add the remaining egg whites. Fold gently until just combined, smooth, and airy. Transfer the batter to the prepared pan and very gently smooth the top into an even layer with an offset spatula.

Bake the cake for 8 to 12 minutes, until it begins to pull away from the sides of the pan. Keep a keen eye on it the whole time to avoid overbaking. You can also test for doneness by gently pressing in the center with your finger: If the cake springs back, it is done.

Transfer the pan to a cooling rack and cool for 10 minutes. Run a knife under hot water, wipe dry, then run the knife around the edges of the still-warm cake. Using a small fine-mesh sieve or small handheld sifter, sift 1 tablespoon of the confectioners' sugar over the cake. Drape a very thin dish towel over the cake, then place a half sheet pan right side up on top of the tea towel. With a quick motion, invert the cake onto the back of the clean sheet pan, and remove the baking pan. Gently remove the parchment paper. Sift the remaining 1 tablespoon of confectioners' sugar over the cake. Trim a scant ¼ inch (6 mm) off all sides of the cake. Starting with a short side, roll the cake up ever so gently, using the towel to support the cake as you go (it's almost like a lift and turn motion)—the towel itself will roll up in the cake. Let the cake cool all rolled up in the towel for at least 20 minutes, seam side down.

MAKE THE FILLING

Pour the cream into the bowl of a stand mixer and refrigerate the bowl for 5 minutes.

Place the bowl on the stand mixer fitted with the whisk attachment. Beat on high speed for 1 minute, then add the confectioners' sugar and vanilla. Continue beating until medium peaks form. Refrigerate until you are ready to assemble.

ASSEMBLE THE HOHO CAKE (PART I)

Unroll the cake gently onto a sheet of parchment on a flat surface. Spread the filling over the cake in an even layer. Gently roll the cake back up, as tightly as possible (use the towel to help guide the cake if needed, but do not roll the towel into the cake). Place the cake, seam side down, on a parchment paper–lined plate or a half sheet pan, cover gently with plastic wrap, and refrigerate for 1 hour to set.

recipe continues next page

SURE THING NOTE

Swiss roll cakes might appear complicated, but the components are all easy to make. Don't obsess over a cake that cracks during the roll. It is easily covered up, and it tastes every bit as good as a cake that rolls perfectly.

FOR THE GANACHE:

4 ounces (120 g) dark chocolate, 60 to 75 percent cacao, coarsely chopped

¾ cup (175 ml) heavy cream

1 teaspoon honey

MAKE THE GANACHE

Melt the chocolate in a microwave-safe glass measuring cup or in the top of a double boiler (see Helpful Hints, page 33). Measure out your heavy cream in a microwave-safe bowl. Add the melted chocolate and honey. In short, 30-second bursts, microwave on medium, stirring in between each burst, until the mixture is smooth and glossy.

ASSEMBLE THE HOHO CAKE (PART 2)

Pour the ganache over the center top of the cake. It should run down evenly over the sides. I like to leave the ends exposed, but you can gently nudge it into place with an offset spatula. Return the cake to the refrigerator for 20 minutes to set the ganache.

Note: You will have some pooled ganache around the bottom of the cake. Use a knife to "break" the ganache away from the cake for a cleaner appearance. The leftover ganache can be rewarmed and used to pour over the sliced HoHo cake (as in the photo) or save it for another application.

Slice and serve directly from the refrigerator. The cake will keep, wrapped gently, in the refrigerator for up to 3 days, but it usually tastes best within 24 to 48 hours.

BLUEBERRY POUND CAKE *with* BLUEBERRY FROSTING

SERVES 9

The eternal pound cake, as glorious as it is in its untouched-by-time state, is made exquisitely better with a fistful of blueberries and dressed in a ridiculous blueberry frosting. Pound cake, a recipe derived from a simple ingredient list made up of one pound each of butter, sugar, flour, and eggs, has existed for ages and is usually delightfully dense to capture a sugary syrup concoction of berries, caramel, or ice cream. My pound cake is less dense. It is not light exactly, but it is fluffier. The blueberries are suspended throughout and it is lovely—almost muffin-like. You could almost skip the frosting. I say almost, because the frosting is a circus of butter, sugar, and blueberries and is light and pleasing and, naturally, purple. Pile it high for some drama. I would like to call out that this was a favorite recipe among tasters and testers alike.

FOR THE BLUEBERRY POUND CAKE:

- 2 cups (240 g) plus 1 tablespoon all-purpose flour
- 1 cup (145 g) fresh or frozen blueberries
- ¼ teaspoon baking soda
- ½ teaspoon kosher salt
- 4 ounces (8 tablespoons / 115 g) unsalted butter, softened
- 1½ cups (300 g) granulated sugar
- 3 large eggs
- 1½ teaspoons pure vanilla extract
- 1 cup (230 g) full-fat plain Greek yogurt, at room temperature

MAKE THE BLUEBERRY POUND CAKE

Preheat the oven to 350°F (180°C) and position a rack in the center. Spray the sides and bottom of a 9 by 5 by 3-inch (23 by 13 by 7.5-cm) loaf pan with nonstick baking spray. Line the bottom with parchment paper and spray the paper.

In a separate medium bowl, toss the berries with the 1 tablespoon of flour until they are very lightly coated. Set aside.

In a medium bowl, whisk together the remaining 2 cups (240 g) of flour, the baking soda, and salt. Set aside.

In the bowl of a stand mixer fitted with the paddle attachment, beat the butter and granulated sugar on medium speed until light and creamy, about 3 minutes. Scrape down the sides and bottom of the bowl and add the eggs, one at a time, scraping down the bowl between each addition. Add the vanilla. Beat on medium speed for about 1 minute or until combined.

Add the flour mixture and the yogurt in two additions, beating in between each addition until just incorporated. Scrape the bottom of the bowl and mix again for 30 seconds.

Remove the bowl from the mixer, scrape down the bowl, and gently fold in the flour-coated blueberries. Scrape the batter into the prepared pan and smooth the top.

recipe continues next page

FOR THE BLUEBERRY FROSTING:

2 ounces (4 tablespoons / 55 g) unsalted butter, softened

2 cups (250 g) confectioners' sugar, plus more if needed

¼ cup (40 g) fresh or frozen and thawed blueberries, plus additional berries to decorate

1 to 2 tablespoons full-fat plain Greek yogurt

Blue food coloring (optional)

Bake for 55 to 65 minutes, until a toothpick inserted in the center of the cake comes out clean. The cake will be deep golden brown.

Allow the cake to cool in the pan for 20 to 30 minutes before inverting onto a wire rack to cool completely.

MAKE THE BLUEBERRY FROSTING

In the bowl of a stand mixer fitted with the paddle attachment, cream the butter on medium speed until smooth. Add about 1 cup (125 g) of the confectioners' sugar and mix on the lowest setting for a minute or two. Add the remaining 1 cup (125 g) confectioners' sugar and beat on the lowest speed to combine. Note: You will most likely have to scrape the bowl down a few times during mixing. The butter and sugar mixture will not be a smooth frosting at this point; it will look a bit dry and sandy until you add the blueberries. Add the blueberries and mix on low speed for about 20 seconds, before increasing the speed to medium and mixing until the mixture starts to look thick and smooth and blue, about 2 minutes.

Add 1 tablespoon of the Greek yogurt and beat on high for 3 to 5 minutes, until the frosting starts to look light and fluffy and holds its shape well. If the frosting looks runny, add confectioners' sugar, 1 tablespoon at a time, until you get the desired thickness. If it looks too dry, add the extra tablespoon of Greek yogurt. If you want to boost the color of the frosting, feel free to add a drop of the blue food coloring.

Spread evenly over the top (and, if you like, sides) of the cooled pound cake, and top with extra blueberries, if desired. Allow the frosting to set by popping it in the fridge for a few minutes before slicing and serving.

The cake will keep in an airtight container at room temperature for up to 3 days.

SURE THING NOTE

I have tried this recipe with both frozen and fresh blueberries, and there is not a lot of variation in the final outcome. However, if you are using frozen blueberries in the frosting, dab away the excess moisture from the berries once thawed for better results.

Sprinkle Berry PARTY CAKE A SUMMER SHEET CAKE

SERVES 12 TO 16

While sprinkles very rarely elevate the taste of any cake, it's hard to deny their visual flair. I am a sucker for a sheet cake studded with colorful sprinkles and topped with a fluffy and cool whipped cream–type frosting. It's the type of cake that embodies laid-back summer vibes. This cake is exactly that summer staple, and it turns out, I quite like to toss in a few seasonal berries to the batter (blueberries and blackberries work exceptionally well) to amp up that summer feeling. It's an easy recipe that works equally well with and without the seasonal berries. It is moist and light, and the frosting—which is a tad more finicky than the cake itself—is airy, silky, and the perfect accompaniment to this summery cake.

FOR THE CAKE:

- 4 cups (12 ounces / 340 g) fresh or frozen blueberries or blackberries, or a mix of both, plus more fresh berries for decorating
- 2½ cups (300 g) plus 2 tablespoons all-purpose flour
- 1 teaspoon baking powder
- ¼ teaspoon baking soda
- ½ teaspoon kosher salt
- 8 ounces (16 tablespoons / 225 g) unsalted butter, softened
- 2 cups (400 g) granulated sugar
- 3 large eggs, at room temperature
- 2 large egg whites, at room temperature
- 2 teaspoons pure vanilla extract
- 1 cup (240 ml) full-fat buttermilk, at room temperature
- 1 cup (240 g) plus 1 tablespoon rainbow sprinkles

MAKE THE CAKE

Preheat the oven to 350°F (180°C) and position a rack in the center. Butter the sides and bottom of a light-colored metal 9 by 13-inch (24 by 36-cm) pan. Line with parchment paper so that it overhangs by about 1 inch (2.5 cm) on two sides of the pan. Butter the paper.

In a medium bowl, toss the berries with the 2 tablespoons of flour until they are very lightly coated. Set aside.

In a separate medium bowl, whisk together the remaining 2½ cups (300 g) flour, the baking powder, baking soda, and salt. Set aside.

In the bowl of a stand mixer fitted with the paddle attachment, beat the butter and granulated sugar on medium speed until light and fluffy, about 5 to 6 minutes. Add the eggs and egg whites, one at a time, beating well after each addition. Scrape down the sides and bottom of the bowl and beat again for 30 to 45 seconds.

Add half of the flour mixture to the creamed butter mixture. Turn the mixer to the lowest setting and beat for 20 to 30 seconds. Add the vanilla and buttermilk all at once and beat for another 20 to 30 seconds. Scrape the bottom and sides of the bowl and add the remaining flour mixture and beat (again, on the lowest setting) until just combined. Run the mixer on medium speed to make sure it is lump free.

FOR THE WHIPPED CREAM FROSTING:

- 8 ounces (225 g) cream cheese, at room temperature
- ¾ cup (90 g) confectioners' sugar, divided
- 2 cups (475 ml) heavy whipping cream, chilled
- 1 teaspoon pure vanilla extract

Remove the bowl from the mixer. Scoop out roughly 1 cup of frosting into the pan and spread it into an even layer to seal the bottom of the pan.

Add the berries and ½ cup (240 g) of the sprinkles all at once into the remaining batter. Using a rubber spatula, gently fold in the berries and sprinkles. Go slow to avoid crushing the berries. Pour the batter into the prepared pan and smooth out the top.

Bake for 45 to 55 minutes, until a toothpick inserted into the center of the cakes comes out clean.

Remove from the oven, place on a cooling rack, and let the cake cool completely. Use a small paring knife to release the cake from the sides of the pan and pull straight up on the parchment to remove it from the pan and place the cake on a large serving platter.

MAKE THE WHIPPED CREAM FROSTING

In the bowl of a stand mixer fitted with the paddle attachment, beat the cream cheese and ¼ cup (30 g) of the confectioners' sugar on high speed until the cream cheese is smooth, ribbony, and creamy. Set aside.

I whip the next part of this recipe by hand to limit the chaos in the kitchen. However, you can absolutely whip the heavy cream and remaining sugar in a stand mixer. If doing so, you will need to place the cream cheese mixture into another medium bowl to set aside and clean out the stand mixing bowl before moving onto the step below.

In a medium mixing bowl, vigorously whisk the heavy cream and the remaining ½ cup (60 g) of confectioners' sugar until it starts to thicken. Whip the mixture until soft peaks form. Add the vanilla and continue beating just until a stiff peak starts to form. (Note: You want to avoid overwhipping at this point.) Gently fold the whipped cream into the cream cheese mixture until fully combined. Be careful not to overmix, you want to maintain the whipped texture.

Frost the cooled cake. Decorate the cake with additional fresh berries and the remaining 1 tablespoon of sprinkles. Refrigerate the cake until you're ready to serve.

The cake will keep tightly covered in the refrigerator for up to 3 days. Slice and serve while cool or at room temperature.

SURE THING NOTES

Two quick things. One, the berries definitely change the cake from more of a birthday-style cake to a fun and quirky summer sheet cake. If you are aiming for a more low-key classic birthday celebration, you can leave out the berries entirely without changing the batter recipe. Two, the icing is truly addictive and worthwhile, but make sure your cream cheese is really at room temperature before starting.

Easy BIRTHDAY CUPCAKES

MAKES 18 CUPCAKES

I was never a cupcake obsessive. Even during the cupcake boom times, when many bakeries opened their doors with an eye to emulating some of the success of Manhattan's Magnolia Bakery, I stayed on the cupcake sidelines a bit, preferring cake slices instead. With the cupcake fad long gone, I have revisited the iconic cupcake with somewhat less jaded eyes. It really is a perfect dessert. I just happen to like them less fussy and less cute than what they became. These birthday cupcakes are fail-safe. They are moist and delicate, but they won't crumble when you peel off the wrapper. You can dress them up with almost any frosting, though I love the sticky sweet chocolate version included here. I highly recommend piling the chocolate frosting high—so from the side it looks as tall as the cupcake itself.

FOR THE SOUR CREAM YELLOW CUPCAKES:

1½ cups (190 g) all-purpose flour

1 teaspoon cornstarch

1½ teaspoons baking powder

½ teaspoon baking soda

½ teaspoon kosher salt

1 cup (200 g) granulated sugar

4 ounces (8 tablespoons / 115 g) unsalted butter, softened, cut into ½-inch cubes

1 tablespoon vegetable oil (or another neutral oil like canola or sunflower oil)

2 large eggs

1 egg yolk

1 teaspoon pure vanilla extract

½ cup (120 g) sour cream

½ cup (120 ml) whole milk

MAKE THE SOUR CREAM YELLOW CUPCAKES

Preheat the oven to 350°F (180°C) and position a rack in the center. Line two cupcake pans with 18 cupcake liners.

In the bowl of a stand mixer fitted with the paddle attachment, mix together the flour, cornstarch, baking powder, baking soda, salt, and granulated sugar until combined. Add the butter and oil and beat until the mixture looks like a sandy, coarse cornmeal and no visible butter clumps remain.

Add the eggs, egg yolk, and vanilla and beat on medium speed until the mixture is thick and smooth. Add the sour cream and turn the mixer to its slowest setting. Slowly stream in the milk, stopping the mixer one or two times to scrape the sides and bottom of the mixing bowl, then increase the speed to medium and beat until mixture is smooth and uniform. Fill the cupcake liners with batter until about two-thirds full. I use a small ice cream scoop with a release mechanism to make the filling process less messy.

Bake for 20 to 25 minutes, rotating the pans halfway through the baking time, until a toothpick inserted in the center of a cupcake comes out clean. Transfer the pans to a wire rack and let cool for 20 minutes. Remove the cupcakes from the pans and place them on the rack to cool completely before frosting.

FOR THE CHOCOLATE FROSTING:

4 ounces (115 g) unsweetened or very dark chocolate, at least 75 percent cacao, coarsely chopped

4 ounces (8 tablespoons / 115 g) unsalted butter, softened

2 cups (250 g) confectioners' sugar, plus more as needed

2 tablespoons heavy cream

1 teaspoon pure vanilla extract

Pinch kosher salt

Rainbow or chocolate sprinkles for topping

MAKE THE CHOCOLATE FROSTING

Melt the chocolate until smooth using either the double-boiler method or microwave method on page 33. Set aside to cool.

In the bowl of a stand mixer fitted with the paddle attachment, beat the butter on medium speed until very smooth and creamy, 2 to 3 minutes. Add the confectioners' sugar and 1 tablespoon of the heavy cream and beat until combined. Slowly stream in the cooled and melted chocolate and continue mixing on low speed until the chocolate and butter are well combined. Add the vanilla, salt, and the remaining tablespoon of heavy cream and beat on medium-high speed until thick but spreadable. If the frosting seems too loose, add additional confectioners' sugar, 1 tablespoon at a time, until it becomes thicker.

Once all the ingredients are well combined, increase the mixer speed to medium-high and continue mixing for an additional 1 to 2 minutes, until the frosting is light and fluffy.

ASSEMBLE THE CUPCAKES

Use an offset spatula or piping bag fitted with a large pastry tip to frost the cupcakes. Decorate as desired with rainbow or chocolate sprinkles.

SURE THING NOTE

Almost every cupcake recipe will tell you that they last up to 3 days, tightly covered, but I truly think most cupcakes—including these—are best served within 24 to 48 hours at most.

A GOOD NEIGHBOR CAKE:

CARAMEL CAKE *with Caramel Frosting*

SERVES 12

My caramel cake with caramel frosting recipe has been bouncing around with me for a few years in various formats (as cupcakes, layer cake, sheet cake), but ultimately this one layer cake pleases me the most, both visually and taste-wise. The cake sponge itself is delicious. While it might be a bit of a stretch to call it "caramel," the brown sugar and lack of vanilla allows for a subtle molasses flavor to peek through. The crumb is tight but not dense, and the overall sponge is a beautiful golden color. However, the real reason to make this cake is the frosting. The brown sugar "caramel" adds such a wonderfully unique dimension to the typical tangy cream cheese frosting, and it is lush and silky and borderline seductive. This is the kind of cake you would bring to your favorite neighbor, because if you don't—if you were to leave this in your house unattended—you are liable to eat the whole thing yourself.

FOR THE CARAMEL CAKE:

- 3 ounces (6 tablespoons / 90 g) unsalted butter, softened, cut into ½-inch cubes
- ¾ cup plus 2 tablespoons (175 g) granulated sugar
- ¼ cup firmly packed (55 g) light brown sugar
- 2 large eggs
- 1¼ cups (160 g) all-purpose flour
- ⅔ cup (160 ml) full-fat buttermilk
- 1 teaspoon baking soda
- 1 tablespoon white vinegar

MAKE THE CARAMEL CAKE

Preheat the oven to 350°F (180°C) and position a rack in the center. Butter the sides and bottom of one 9-inch (23-cm) round cake pan and line the bottom with parchment paper. Butter the paper.

In the bowl of a stand mixer fitted with the paddle attachment, beat the butter on medium speed until creamy, about 1 minute. Add the granulated and brown sugars and beat until light and fluffy, about 3 minutes. Scrape down the sides and bottom of the bowl and add the eggs, one at a time, beating well after each addition. Scrape down the bowl again and add the flour and buttermilk. Beat on the lowest setting until combined.

In a small bowl or cup, dissolve the baking soda in the vinegar and stir it into the batter until just combined. Pour the batter into the prepared pan and smooth the top.

Bake for 25 to 35 minutes, until a toothpick inserted in the center of the cake comes out clean. The cake top will be slightly browned.

recipe continues next page

FOR THE CARAMEL FROSTING:

2 tablespoons firmly packed dark brown sugar

2½ ounces (5 tablespoons / 75 g) unsalted butter, softened, cut into ½-inch cubes and divided into tablespoons

3 tablespoons heavy cream

4 ounces (115 g) cream cheese, at room temperature

¼ teaspoon kosher salt

1 cup (125 g) confectioners' sugar, plus more as needed

Chocolate chips, chocolate pearls, or rainbow sprinkles for decorating (optional)

Transfer the cake to a wire rack and let cool for 30 minutes. Invert the cake onto the rack, remove the pan, remove the parchment, and invert the cake again so the top is facing upward. Let cool completely while you make the frosting.

MAKE THE CARAMEL FROSTING

In a small saucepan over medium heat, stir together the brown sugar and 2 tablespoons of the butter until melted and combined. Bring the mixture to a boil and boil for 10 to 15 seconds. Remove from the heat, whisk in the heavy cream, and transfer the mixture to a bowl to cool completely. (Note: You can stir or whisk the mixture vigorously to release excess heat or, to cool the mixture quickly for immediate use, you can nestle the bowl with the mixture in a larger bowl filled halfway with ice.)

Once the brown sugar mixture is nearly cool, put the remaining 3 tablespoons of butter in the bowl of a stand mixer fitted with the paddle attachment and beat on medium speed until it is lump free. Add the cream cheese and salt and continue beating until the mixture is smooth. Scrape down the sides and bottom of the bowl and beat again for 15 seconds. Turn the mixer to low and stream in the brown sugar mixture. Scrape down the bowl again, add the confectioners' sugar all at once, and beat on medium speed until smooth. If the frosting seems too loose, add additional confectioners' sugar, 1 tablespoon at a time, until it becomes thicker. You can also refrigerate the frosting for 10 minutes to let it firm up before frosting.

FROST THE CAKE

Transfer the cake to a serving platter and apply the frosting to the sides and top of the cooled cake. Decorate the cake with chocolate chips, chocolate pearls, or sprinkles, if using.

Refrigerate the cake until you're ready to serve but allow the cake to come almost to room temperature for optimal flavor.

The cake will keep tightly covered in the refrigerator for up to 3 days. Slice and serve while cool or at room temperature.

SURE THING NOTE

There are many instances where light brown sugar and dark brown sugar are basically interchangeable, but I highly recommend only using dark brown in the caramel frosting. I have certainly used light brown in a pinch, and while still superb, it is not quite as transformative as the dark brown version printed here. If you have to make a swap, and only want to buy one type of brown sugar for this recipe, just purchase dark brown and use it in a one-for-one swap in the cake.

CHOCOLATE *Malted* RYE LOAF CAKE *with Ganache*

SERVES 9

I fell hard for a version of this loaf that I first spied in Edinburgh, Scotland. It was being served, in ample slices, alongside near-perfect croissants and tarts, at Lannan Bakery in the leafy neighborhood of Stockbridge—a very pleasant twenty-minute or so walk from the city center. The bakery version of this cake was baked in a Pullman loaf pan which had the effect of creating a very modern, very square, very artistic visual—something I wanted to both eat and covet at the same time. However, you don't need to bake this in a specialized loaf pan to understand why it is so spectacular. Alex Roberts, friend and baker, created this loaf cake version, which is full of immense chocolate flavor without being obscenely rich—not an easy feat. True, the ganache is a bit over the top, but it adds more than just chocolate, it adds a contrasting layer of chocolate and texture that pulls the whole thing together.

FOR THE CHOCOLATE RYE LOAF:

- ⅓ cup (30 g) unsweetened dark cocoa powder
- ⅓ cup very hot water
- 1 cup (125 g) rye flour
- ½ cup (65 g) all-purpose flour
- 2 tablespoons malted milk powder
- 1½ teaspoons baking powder
- ¾ teaspoon baking soda
- ½ teaspoon kosher salt
- 1 large egg, at room temperature
- 1 egg yolk, at room temperature
- ¾ cup (150 g) granulated sugar
- ½ cup packed (110 g) light brown sugar
- ⅓ cup (80 ml) vegetable oil (or a neutral oil like canola or sunflower oil)
- 1 teaspoon pure vanilla extract
- 1 cup (240 ml) whole milk, at room temperature

MAKE THE CHOCOLATE RYE LOAF

Preheat the oven to 350°F (180°C) and position a rack in the center. Spray the sides and bottom of a 9 by 5 by 3-inch (23 by 13 by 7.5-cm) loaf pan with nonstick baking spray. Line the bottom with parchment paper so that it overhangs the long sides of the pan by about 1 inch. Spray the parchment.

In a small bowl, whisk together the cocoa powder and hot water. Set aside.

In a large bowl, whisk together the rye and all-purpose flours, malted milk powder, baking powder, baking soda, and salt. Set aside.

In the bowl of a stand mixer fitted with the whisk attachment, beat the egg, egg yolk, and the granulated and brown sugars on high speed until light and pale, 1 to 2 minutes. Turn the mixer to low speed and stream in the oil. Stop the mixer, scrape down the sides and bottom of the bowl, and add the vanilla and the cocoa mixture. Mix on medium speed to combine. Add half of the flour mixture and half of the milk and mix on low speed until just combined. Add the remaining flour mixture and the remaining milk and mix again on low speed until just combined. Remove the bowl from the mixer and, using a rubber spatula, scrape down the bottom and sides of the bowl and fold in any remaining dry ingredients. Scrape the batter into the prepared pan and smooth the top.

recipe continues next page

FOR THE GANACHE TOPPING:

2½ ounces (75 g) dark chocolate, 60 to 75 percent cacao, coarsely chopped

¼ cup (60 ml) heavy cream

1 teaspoon honey

Bake for 50 to 60 minutes, or until a toothpick inserted in the middle of the cake comes out mostly clean. Note: This cake is super fudgy, and the tried-and-true toothpick test can sometimes be misleading. If the toothpick emerges with a few moist crumbs, that is okay. It just shouldn't be wet.

Let the cake cool in the pan on a wire rack for 30 minutes. Use a small paring knife to loosen the cake from the sides of the pan. Invert the cake to remove it before placing it back onto the wire rack to cool completely.

MAKE THE GANACHE TOPPING

Melt the chocolate in the microwave in a microwave-safe bowl as on page 33. Add the heavy cream and honey. In short 30-second bursts of the microwave on medium and stirring in between each burst, heat until the mixture is smooth and glossy.

Pour the ganache down the center of the cake and use an offset spatula to nudge the ganache toward and over the edges for a drip effect. Pop the loaf cake into the refrigerator for about 10 minutes to set the ganache before slicing and serving.

The cake will keep at room temperature (or in the refrigerator), tightly covered, for up to 3 days.

SURE THING NOTES

This is a rich chocolate cake, and I usually temper it with freshly whipped cream or vanilla gelato. This is also a cake that freezes beautifully for dessert emergencies (unexpected company). Simply wrap the unglazed cake tightly in plastic and/or tinfoil until needed. Then bring it to room temperature and dress with ganache.

EASY OLIVE OIL ORANGE CAKE

SERVES 12 TO 16

This is the least fussy Bundt cake you will ever meet. The fact that it happens to be glorious—tender-crumbed and bursting with fruity olive oil notes and light and zingy from the orange zest—is a bonus. This cake is an adaptation of an adaptation of a recipe that appeared in one of the Baked cookbooks, but this version is less particular, less nitpicky. It has been engineered to be quick and delicious, without a lot of mess. I even took pains to eliminate extra bowls and steps because my current lifestyle choices allow for more ambiguity. I even gave up measuring zest. It seemed silly and misguided. Just add the zest of two oranges and relax. The amount will change every single time based on the size of the oranges, but it will be delicious every single time.

- 3 cups (375 g) all-purpose flour
- 1 tablespoon baking powder
- ½ teaspoon kosher salt
- 4 large eggs
- 2 cups (400 g) granulated sugar
- 1 cup (240 ml) full-fat buttermilk
- 1 cup (240 ml) extra-virgin olive oil
- Freshly grated zest of 2 oranges
- 1½ teaspoons pure vanilla extract
- Confectioners' sugar for dusting (optional)

Preheat the oven to 350°F (180°C) and position a rack in the center. Butter and flour a 10 to 12-cup (2.4 to 2.8-L) Bundt pan so that flour covers most of the pan. (See page 31 for how to prepare a Bundt pan.)

In a medium bowl, whisk together the flour, baking powder, and salt. Set aside.

In a large mixing bowl, whisk together the eggs and granulated sugar until well combined. Then whisk vigorously for a minute or two, until the mixture is very light and pale yellow. Add the buttermilk, olive oil, zest (you can zest the oranges directly over the mixture to save another bowl or plate to clean), and vanilla. Whisk the mixture until well blended.

Add the dry ingredients all at once. With a wooden spoon or spatula, stir (don't beat) until all the ingredients are incorporated. Pour the batter into the prepared pan.

Bake for 40 to 50 minutes, until a toothpick or skewer inserted into the middle of the Bundt comes out with moist crumbs. Check in on this cake on the earlier side as the baking time varies quite a bit, and it can go from beautiful and moist to beautiful and a bit dry quickly.

recipe continues next page

SURE THING NOTE

Allow me a moment to again praise Nate Stearns, recipe tester extraordinaire, for his amazing suggestion to glaze this cake. While most olive oil cakes are sans glaze, I really think you should try his simple citrus glaze on this cake for an over-the-top citrus punch. He even polled his co-workers on how to serve the cake: glaze or no glaze. Glaze won by a wide margin.

Remove the Bundt pan from the oven and cool for 15 minutes. Gently loosen the sides of the cake from the pan and turn it out onto a cooling rack with the decorative side up. Cool completely.

Dust with confectioners' sugar before serving or top with Nate's Citrus Glaze.

The cake can be stored tightly covered at room temperature for up to 3 days.

NATE'S SIMPLE CITRUS GLAZE

- 2 tablespoons unsalted butter, melted
- 2 tablespoons heavy cream
- Zest of ½ orange
- 2 tablespoons fresh squeezed orange juice (juice from approximately 1 orange)
- 1½ cups (200 g) confectioners' sugar (plus more as needed)

In a bowl, whisk together the melted butter, heavy cream, orange zest, and orange juice. Add the confectioners' sugar and whisk until a semi-thick and pourable glaze forms. If it feels too thin, keep adding confectioners' sugar, 1 tablespoon at a time, until it thickens up.

Slowly pour the frosting over the crown of the Bundt cake in a few ribbony layers. Let the frosting set before serving.

Whiskey COCOA BUNDT CAKE

SERVES 12 TO 16

This cake has been with me through a few iterations. Almost all of them involve a whiskey of sorts. It is a big, beautiful, and bold cake. While the steps are relatively straightforward, it does involve a few more than the average recipe in this book. But it is worth every dirty bowl you have to clean. The cake itself is the exact ideal of what you imagine a chocolate cake to taste like—moist, delicate but not too delicate, rich, and deep in chocolaty flavor. The whiskey in the cake is not necessarily pungent and neither is the fruity olive oil since the chocolate flavor is so forward. They are mere background players to the main event. However, it is in the glaze where the buttery whiskey flavor shines. This glaze features a heavy pour, so feel free to cut back if you aren't big on that buzzy hit. And while the glaze is divine, it is entirely fine to skip it. Just dust with Dutch-process cocoa powder (as in the photo on page 166) to finish with something more subtle, less sweet, and alcohol-free.

FOR THE CAKE:

¾ cup (60 g) unsweetened dark Dutch-process cocoa powder (Valrhona is recommended), plus more for dusting the pan

¼ cup (20 g) unsweetened black cocoa powder

½ cup (120 ml) hot brewed coffee

½ cup (120 ml) bourbon (I like Basil Hayden) or whiskey

2¼ cups (285 g) all-purpose flour

2 teaspoons baking powder

1¼ teaspoons kosher salt

½ teaspoon baking soda

2¼ cups packed (495 g) dark brown sugar

½ cup plus 2 tablespoons (150 ml) neutral oil (like vegetable or canola)

¼ cup (60 ml) extra-virgin olive oil

1 tablespoon pure vanilla extract

2 large eggs

2 egg yolks

1½ cups (340 g) full-fat plain Greek yogurt

MAKE THE CAKE

Preheat the oven to 350°F (175°C) and position a rack in the center. Butter the inside of a 10 to 12-cup (2.8-L) Bundt pan, dust with 2 to 3 tablespoons of cocoa powder, and knock out the excess. Alternatively, liberally apply a nonstick baking spray, dust with cocoa, and knock out the excess. Either way, make sure the pan's nooks and crannies are all thoroughly coated.

In a medium-size heatproof bowl, combine the dark and black cocoa powders. Pour the hot coffee directly over the powders and whisk until well blended. Whisk in the bourbon. Set aside to cool.

In a large bowl, whisk together the flour, baking powder, salt, and baking soda. Set aside.

In another large bowl, whisk the brown sugar, neutral, and olive oils, and vanilla until combined. Add the eggs and egg yolks and whisk again until just combined. Add the flour mixture in three parts, alternating with the cocoa mixture, beginning and ending with the flour mixture. Whisk each addition gently to combine.

Fold one-third of the yogurt into the batter to lighten it. Fold in half of the remaining yogurt until just incorporated, then fold in the rest until no streaks remain. Pour the batter into the prepared pan.

recipe continues next page

FOR THE BUTTER WHISKEY GLAZE:

- 1½ ounces (3 tablespoons / 42 g) unsalted butter
- 2 tablespoons heavy cream
- 2¼ to 2¾ cups (235 to 290 g) confectioners' sugar, sifted
- 3 tablespoons good-quality whiskey
- Chocolate sprinkles (optional)

Bake for 50 to 55 minutes, until a small sharp knife or toothpick inserted into the center comes out with just a few moist crumbs. Transfer the pan to a wire rack to cool completely.

Gently loosen the sides of the cake from the pan and turn it out onto the rack so that the crown is facing up. Place a baking sheet (lined with parchment, if you like, for ease of cleaning) underneath the wire rack.

MAKE THE BUTTER WHISKEY GLAZE

In a small saucepan, melt the butter over low heat. Remove from the heat and whisk in the cream. Add ¾ cup (95 g) of the confectioners' sugar and whisk to combine. Repeat with another ¾ cup (95 g) and whisk to combine. Repeat with another ¾ cup (95 g) and whisk to combine. Add the whiskey and whisk until uniform. The glaze should be thick and ropy, but pourable—not runny and thin. If the glaze looks too thin, add the remaining ½ cup (65 g) of confectioners' sugar and whisk to combine.

GLAZE THE BLACK COCOA BUNDT

Pour the glaze over the room-temperature cake in thick ribbons; it will slowly drip down the sides. Add a few sprinkles to the top, if using. Let set for about 15 minutes before serving.

The cake will keep in an airtight container at room temperature for up to 3 days.

SURE THING NOTE

Don't have black cocoa powder? It's fine. Just substitute Dutch-process cocoa powder one for one in the recipe. The black cocoa powder provides more of a visual accent—it makes the cake an inky midnight black that contrasts beautifully with the white icing—than it is a taste modifier.

MARBLE LOAF CAKE *with* PECAN TOPPING

SERVES 9

If you happen to be partial to marble loaves, we should probably be fast friends. While they are not properly celebrated in the bakery world, they are nimble little beasts doing double-duty as both a morning treat and afternoon snack and everything in between. I am aware that they have gained some continued recognition as being one of Starbucks' original pastry-case offerings, and I have nothing but praise for the moist Starbucks version. But this marble cake is the next level. The chocolate swirl is made with chocolate, not cocoa, which amplifies the contrast between the batters. And for kicks, I cap off my marble loaf with a nutty pecan topping for both crunch and flavor.

FOR THE PECAN TOPPING:

3 tablespoons pecans, coarsely chopped

1 tablespoon light brown sugar, firmly packed

Pinch ground cinnamon

FOR THE CHOCOLATE SWIRL:

2 ounces (55 g) dark chocolate, 60 to 75 percent cacao, coarsely chopped

FOR THE SOUR CREAM CAKE:

1¾ cups (225 g) all-purpose flour

1 teaspoon baking powder

1 teaspoon baking soda

½ teaspoon kosher salt

4 ounces (8 tablespoons / 115 g) unsalted butter at room temperature

1¼ cup (225 g) granulated sugar

2 large eggs, at room temperature

8 ounces (225 g) sour cream, at room temperature

1½ teaspoons pure vanilla extract

MAKE THE PECAN TOPPING

Use the tips of your fingers to stir together the pecans, brown sugar, and cinnamon.

MAKE THE CHOCOLATE SWIRL

Melt the chocolate until smooth using either the double-boiler method or microwave method on page 33. The melted chocolate should be placed in a medium-sized bow and set aside.

MAKE THE SOUR CREAM CAKE

Preheat the oven to 350°F (180°C) and position a rack in the center. Line the bottom with parchment paper so that it overhangs the long sides of the pan by about 1 inch. Spray the parchment.

In a medium bowl, whisk the flour, baking powder, baking soda, and salt together. Set aside.

In the bowl of a stand mixer fitted with the paddle attachment, cream the butter on medium speed until smooth and ribbonlike, about 6 to 7 minutes. Scrape down the bowl and add the granulated sugar. Beat until the mixture is smooth and fluffy. Add the eggs, one at a time, beating well after each addition. Scrape down the bowl and mix for 30 seconds. Add the sour cream and vanilla and beat just until incorporated. Add the dry ingredients in two additions, scraping down the bowl before each addition and beating only until each addition is just incorporated. Do not overmix.

recipe continues next page

Scoop out one-third of the cake batter and add to the melted chocolate. Use a spatula to combine the chocolate and the batter to make a smooth chocolate batter.

Spread half of the remaining plain cake batter in the prepared pan. Use an ice-cream scoop with a release mechanism to dollop alternating chocolate and plain batter directly on top of the plain batter in a checkerboard pattern. It does not have to be perfect, and do not use all the plain batter. The dollops will touch and mostly cover the plain batter, but some plain batter will peek through. Use a butter knife to swirl the chocolate and plain batter together. Scoop out the remaining plain cake batter and dollop it on top of the checkerboard swirl; smooth the top. Use a butter knife and swirl it through the batter, making rounded circles from one side of the pan to the other. Sprinkle the pecan topping in an even layer on top of the cake batter.

Bake for 45 to 55 minutes, until a sharp knife inserted in the center of the cake comes out clean.

Remove from the oven and let the cake cool in the pan on a wire rack for 30 minutes. Use a small paring knife to loosen the cake from the sides of the pan and invert the cake onto the wire rack and invert again so the pecan top is up.

Serve warm or at room temperature.

The cake will keep tightly covered at room temperature for 3 days.

SURE THING NOTE

The layering and swirling of the batters in the directions might be a bit overcomplicated, but if you are in a rush or simply can't be bothered, you can easily achieve an equally beautiful swirl by just spooning random chocolate and vanilla batter into the prepared pan at will, but make sure you start with a base layer of vanilla batter. You will still swirl through the mixtures with a knife, but you can forgo the ice-cream scoop precision.

Cream Cheese BANANA BREAD

SERVES 9

I am always surprised how a simple slice of banana bread can improve my mood. It's not an obvious pick-me-up—not in the straightforward way a square of chocolate or a chunky cookie is—but it lifts my spirits nonetheless. I have published many banana bread recipes over the years and made many others from various recipes floating about. And, honestly, there is no sense in choosing a favorite when they are all equally pleasing and not too dissimilar. But for this book, I thought it would be fun to marry my fondness for cream cheese with the simple pleasures of banana bread. It is quite good. If you like banana cake and you like cream cheese frosting, you will absolutely love this banana bread.

FOR THE CREAM CHEESE FILLING:

- 8 ounces (225 g) full-fat cream cheese, at room temperature
- ¼ cup (50 g) granulated sugar
- Pinch fine sea salt
- ¼ cup (60 ml) full-fat buttermilk, at room temperature
- 1 teaspoon pure vanilla extract
- 1 large egg
- 2 tablespoons all-purpose flour

MAKE THE CREAM CHEESE FILLING

In a small bowl, using a wooden spoon, stir together the cream cheese, sugar, and salt until smooth. You will most likely use the back of the spoon to press out lumps between the spoon and side of the bowl. Add the buttermilk, vanilla, and egg and whisk until smooth. Whisk in the flour. The mixture should be smooth, thick, and creamy. Chill the mixture in the refrigerator while you make the banana bread batter. Note: The mixture should be cool, but not cold. Do not refrigerate for more than 20 minutes.

MAKE THE BANANA BREAD

Preheat the oven to 350°F (180° C) and position a rack in the center. Spray the sides and bottom of a 9 by 5 by 3 inch (23 by 13 by 7.5-cm) loaf pan with nonstick baking spray. Line the bottom with parchment paper so that it overhangs the long sides of the pan by about 1 inch. Spray the parchment.

In a small bowl, whisk together the flour, baking soda, baking powder, salt, cinnamon, and nutmeg. Set aside.

In a large bowl, whisk together the sugar and bananas until smooth (it is fine and even encouraged to have a few random banana bits after whisking). Whisk in the buttermilk, oil, and vanilla. Whisk until smooth. Add the eggs and whisk to incorporate.

Add the dry mixture to the wet mixture and, using a rubber spatula, gently fold them together until smooth and no flour streaks remain.

recipe continues next page

FOR THE TOFFEE SAUCE:

¾ cup packed (165 g) light brown sugar

1¼ cups (300 ml) heavy cream

2 tablespoons unsalted butter

1 tablespoon unsulfured molasses

¼ teaspoon kosher salt

Bake for 17 to 18 minutes, until a toothpick inserted in the middle of a pudding comes out clean. (Note: It's actually okay to overbake these by a minute or two since they are very sticky.)

MAKE THE TOFFEE SAUCE

As soon as you pop the cakes in the oven, start making the sauce. In a small pot over medium-low heat, combine the brown sugar, heavy cream, butter, molasses, and salt.

While gently stirring, bring the mixture to a simmer. Continue simmering for 5 minutes, until the mixture bubbles and slightly thickens. Set aside.

ASSEMBLE THE STICKY TOFFEE PUDDINGS

Line a baking sheet with parchment paper.

When the mini cakes are done, remove them from the oven, reduce the heat to 300°F (150°C), and allow the mini cakes to cool in the pan for 10 minutes. Pop the mini cakes out onto the parchment paper–lined baking sheet. Wait 3 minutes. Slice each mini cake in half horizontally.

Spoon a tablespoon of toffee sauce into each muffin well. Place the bottom layer of each mini cake into the wells over the sauce. Spoon another tablespoon or more of toffee sauce over each. Place the top of each mini cake over the bottom layer and spoon a tiny teaspoonful of toffee sauce over the top layer to finish. Return the pan to the oven and bake for 6 minutes to warm through.

Remove the pan from the oven and carefully invert the hot pan over the parchment paper–lined baking sheet. Plate each sticky toffee pudding while warm and top with more toffee sauce. If your toffee sauce has thickened while you were assembling the desserts, you can rewarm the mixture until it thins out again.

While not quite as impressive as just from the oven, leftover puddings can be stored tightly covered in the refrigerator. Warm in a microwave (15-second bursts on high until warmed through) or in a 300°F (150°C) oven for 5 minutes.

SURE THING NOTES

Two quick notes here. First, these really should be served warm. Second, even if you are using a nonstick muffin pan, it is essential to prepare it with butter and flour to prevent sticking. Sticky toffee pudding is "sticky," and it is better not to leave it to chance.

MORNING STUFF

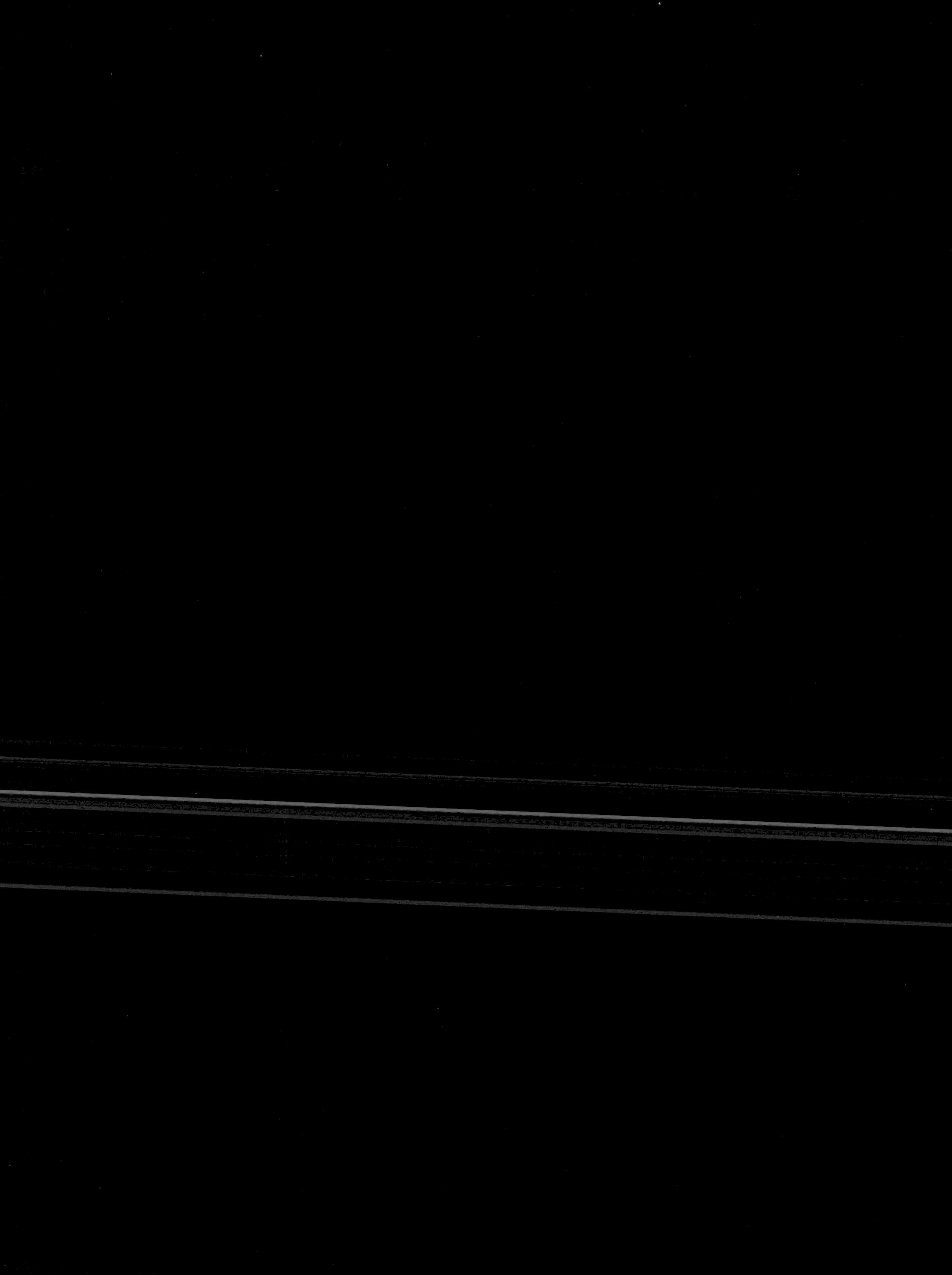

QUICK CORN MUFFINS

MAKES 12 MUFFINS

The beauty of a corn muffin is twofold. First, if you serve them slightly warm from the oven and slather them in honey butter, you will be hard-pressed to find a more perfect way to start your morning. Second, corn muffins become even more special when cooled, sliced, and toasted, making them the ideal "make-ahead" or "leftover" muffin. My preference generally leans toward the toasted method, but I have yet to turn down a just-baked muffin.

FOR THE MUFFINS:

- ¾ cup (120 g) fine cornmeal
- 1 cup (130 g) all-purpose flour
- ¼ cup (50 g) granulated sugar
- 2 tablespoons light brown sugar
- 1 tablespoon baking powder
- ½ teaspoon baking soda
- ½ teaspoon kosher salt
- 1 cup (240 ml) full-fat buttermilk
- 1 tablespoon honey
- 1 large egg
- 2 ounces (4 tablespoons / 55 g) unsalted butter, melted

MAKE THE MUFFINS

Preheat the oven to 400°F (200°C) and position a rack in the center. Grease a standard 12-cup muffin pan with butter, making sure it coats the bottom and sides of each well evenly. Do not use muffin liners.

In a medium bowl, whisk together the cornmeal, flour, granulated and brown sugars, baking powder, baking soda, and salt. Set aside.

In a large liquid measuring cup, measure out the buttermilk and add the honey and egg. Whisk together until combined.

Fold the wet ingredients into the dry ingredients until just blended and a few dry streaks remain. Pour in the melted butter and gently fold until combined.

Divide the batter evenly among the muffin cups so that each well is about three-quarters full. I use a small ice-cream scoop with a release mechanism to make the portioning into cups less messy.

Bake for 14 to 16 minutes, or until the muffins have risen and are golden brown around the edges. Note: I tend to bake these on the longer side for crispier edges.

Remove the muffins from the oven, let them cool for 10 minutes in the pan, then release them onto a wire rack dome side up.

FOR THE HONEY BUTTER:

2 tablespoons unsalted butter, melted

1 tablespoon honey

MAKE THE HONEY BUTTER

While the muffins are baking, in a small cup, stir the melted butter and honey together.

SERVING THE MUFFINS

Use a toothpick to poke three to five holes on the top of each muffin, brush with honey butter, and serve. You should only apply the honey butter just before serving. Do not apply the honey butter to muffins you are storing for serving later.

Wrapped tightly, muffins can be stored for up to 3 days at room temperature. To revive day-old (or older) muffins, slice and toast in a toaster oven or under the broiler before brushing with honey butter and serving.

SURE THING NOTES

This is a straightforward, unfussy, quick, and easy corn muffin recipe that is also insanely delicious. From start to finish, these muffins can be made in under 30 minutes, making them part of a heavy breakfast rotation necessity. Do you need the honey butter? No, but the crevices of a cornmeal-textured muffin create an otherworldly flavor when paired with melted butter.

EVERYBODY *Loves* MONKEY BREAD

SERVES 12 TO 16

Monkey bread is a top-tier crowd pleaser. The piping hot pillowy bites are reminiscent of the best parts of both a cinnamon roll and a yeasted doughnut: gooey, chewy, and warmly spiced. It is the kind of breakfast treat that is both visually appealing—a giant Bundt ring of golden dough balls—and perfectly engineered for large morning gatherings. I tend to make this recipe only when the house is bursting with overnight guests, like the mornings before Thanksgiving and Christmas Eve, but I am trying to break it out of its "special holiday recipe" mold and bake it for more random brunches. It never disappoints. I resurrected this recipe from one of my previous books, but re-engineered it to fit a make-ahead schedule. In my opinion, it's a lower lift to prep everything the night before and bake it off in the morning.

FOR THE MONKEY BREAD

- 1¼ cups whole milk
- 2 teaspoons instant yeast
- 4 cups (520 g) all-purpose flour
- ⅓ cup (65 g) granulated sugar
- 1 teaspoon salt
- 1 large egg
- 2½ ounces (5 tablespoons / 70 g) unsalted butter, melted

To make your morning bake off simple, prepare the monkey bread recipe the night prior. See the Sure Thing Note if you want to make it all in one go.

The night before baking off, line two half sheet baking pans with parchment paper.

In a small saucepan, warm the milk until it is warm—not hot—to the touch. If you have a food thermometer handy, you want to make sure it does not exceed 110°F (43°C), or it will kill the yeast. Remove the pan from the heat and whisk in the yeast until it dissolves.

In the bowl of a stand mixer fitted with the paddle attachment, beat the flour, sugar, and salt to combine.

In a small bowl or cup, beat the egg with a fork and add it to the dry ingredients. Mix on low speed until combined.

Turn the mixer to low and slowly stream in the milk. Keep mixing on the lowest speed until just combined. Turn off the mixer, add the melted butter, and beat again until the dough comes together.

Replace the paddle attachment with the dough hook and continue to mix on medium speed until the dough becomes silky and slightly tacky (not overly sticky), about 8 to 10 minutes. The dough should come together in a mass and will start to pull away from the sides and bottom of the bowl. If the dough looks too wet, toss in a dusting of flour. If it is too dry, add water, 1 teaspoon at a time, until it takes form.

FOR THE CINNAMON-SUGAR COATING

1¼ cups firmly packed (260 g) dark brown sugar

2 teaspoons cinnamon

4 ounces (4 tablespoons / 115 g) unsalted butter, melted and cooled

Generously spray—like really coat every surface—the inside of a 10-inch Bundt pan and a large bowl with nonstick cooking spray.

Place the dough in the bowl and flip it around a few times to make sure the dough is completely covered in the nonstick cooking spray. Cover the bowl with a dish towel and let it rest in a warm area until the dough has doubled in size, approximately 1 hour.

With clean hands, deflate the dough. Remove the dough from the bowl and place on a lightly greased or very lightly floured surface. Pat the dough into a rough 8-inch square, and using a bench knife (or any small blade), cut the dough into 1-inch square pieces (about ½ ounce / 14 g). You should have about 60 squares, but it is not always exact. Roll each piece of dough into a ball and place on the sheet pan.

MAKE THE CINNAMON-SUGAR COATING

In a small bowl, stir together the sugar and cinnamon. Place the melted butter in another small bowl.

ASSEMBLE THE MONKEY BREAD

Dip each ball into the melted butter to coat, then roll the ball in the cinnamon-sugar mixture and place it in the Bundt pan. Continue this process with each ball until you have several layers, arranging each layer like you are building a brick wall.

Cover the pan with plastic and place in the refrigerator overnight (or up to 18 hours).

PREPARE THE MORNING BAKE

Remove the pan from the refrigerator and let it proof for about 1.5 hours. The dough will approximately double in size and appear puffier. Go make your coffee and check your socials while you wait.

Preheat the oven to 350°F (180°C). Bake the Bundt until the top is a deep brown and the sugary caramel coating is bubbling around the edges, about 30 minutes. Remove the pan from the oven and let cool for 5 minutes before turning it out directly onto a serving platter. Serve warm.

Monkey bread is best served directly from the oven. If you have any leftovers, you can store them at room temperature, tightly covered, and reheat in a warm 250°F (120°C) oven until the monkey bread is hot to the touch.

SURE THING NOTE

If you are an early riser and prefer to make this recipe all in one morning, adjust the recipe as follows: Once the monkey bread is assembled, skip the refrigeration step and allow the dough to rise until doubled (since it is not refrigerated, it should only take about 1 hour as opposed to 1.5 hours) before baking.

Hazelnut CHOCOLATE CHIP SCONES WITH NUTELLA GLAZE

MAKES 8 SCONES

Scones, big chunky American-style scones, never quite popped off in the same way as other viral-ready treats. This is a shame. A well-made scone is the ideal companion for tea, coffee, and leisurely morning routines. While they are typically less sweet than their other breakfast pastry brethren like muffins and coffee cake, they still fulfill that "special morning treat" requirement needed to maintain sanity in this not-so-sane world. I assure you, these scones are a double treat. Each wedge is like an oversize hazelnut chip cookie and shortbread hybrid: sweet but flaky and studded with hazelnuts and shaggy bits of chocolate. The Nutella glaze is literally just Nutella, which is exquisite on its own. No need to improve on one of the great gifts of our time. The more glaze the better, in my opinion, so be generous with those zigzags.

FOR THE HAZELNUT CHOCOLATE CHIP SCONES:

- 2 cups (250 g) all-purpose flour
- ⅓ cup (65 g) granulated sugar
- 1½ teaspoons baking powder
- ½ teaspoon baking soda
- ½ teaspoon kosher salt
- 4 ounces (8 tablespoons / 115 g) chilled unsalted butter, cut into ½-inch cubes
- 5 tablespoons (75 ml) full-fat buttermilk
- 1 large egg
- 1 teaspoon pure vanilla extract
- ½ cup (65 g) hazelnuts, toasted, cooled, and coarsely chopped (see Note on page 184)
- ½ cup (85 g) milk chocolate chips or chunks
- 2 tablespoons demerara sugar

MAKE THE HAZELNUT CHOCOLATE CHIP SCONES

In a medium bowl, whisk together the flour, granulated sugar, baking powder, baking soda, and salt. Add the butter. Working quickly, use your fingertips or a pastry cutter to rub (or cut) the butter into the flour mixture until the mixture is coarse and pebbly with a few random larger butter chunks (the texture should not be even).

Measure out 4 tablespoons (60 ml) of the buttermilk into a glass measuring cup. Add the egg and vanilla (this saves washing an extra bowl) and whisk together. Make a well in the dry ingredients and pour in the wet ingredients. Gently knead the dough with your hands until the dough just starts to come together. Add the hazelnuts and milk chocolate chips or chunks and continue to knead gently to incorporate.

recipe continues next page

SURE THING NOTE

If you are feeding hungry family members or overnight guests in the morning, I might suggest mixing the dry ingredients and butter together the night before and storing in the refrigerator until needed. It is not necessary, but it saves a somewhat messy step. Just wake up, add the buttermilk mixture and mix-ins, knead, and bake.

FOR THE NUTELLA GLAZE:

⅓ cup (80 ml) Nutella

Pinch kosher salt

Move the dough to a lightly floured surface. Use your hands to shape and pat the dough into an even-shaped disk about 1 inch (2.5 cm) in height.

Do not overwork the dough. Refrigerate the disk for at least 15 minutes, or about the amount of time it takes for your oven to heat up.

Preheat the oven to 375°F (190°C) and position a rack near the center. Line a half sheet baking pan with parchment paper.

Remove the dough from the refrigerator. Cut the disk into eight equal-size wedges and transfer to the prepared baking sheet. Brush the tops of the scones with the remaining 1 tablespoon of buttermilk and sprinkle with the demerara.

Bake for 16 to 20 minutes, until the scones are golden brown. Transfer the scones to a wire cooling rack to cool completely. Place the baking sheet you just used under the wire rack.

MAKE THE NUTELLA GLAZE

Place the Nutella in a heatproof bowl and microwave in short bursts until soupy. Alternatively, you can heat the Nutella using the double-boiler method on page 33. Once warm and runny, use the tines of a fork or a small spoon to apply the Nutella glaze over the scones in a zigzag motion. Alternatively, you can slice the scones in half horizontally and smear the interior with room-temperature Nutella.

Store the scones in an airtight container for up to 2 days at room temperature, though they are best eaten within 24 hours.

Note: To toast raw hazelnuts, line a baking sheet with parchment paper, spread out the hazelnuts in an even layer, and bake in a preheated oven at 375°F (190°C) for 10 to 13 minutes, until fragrant.

SURE THING NOTE

HOW TO ADD COLD BUTTER TO FLOUR

I have tried a bunch of different methods for incorporating butter into a dry flour mix and, trust me, a pastry cutter is the way to go. Simply add your cold, chunked butter to the mix and cut it into the flour, then return the mix to the refrigerator for 20 to 30 minutes, if you can.

If you don't have a pastry cutter, you can use your fingertips, just be sure not to overwork the butter.

I have also tried using a box grater to grate frozen butter into the mix. While it works fine, I think I still prefer the pastry cutter method. It's faster and easier.

CAST-IRON ORANGE *Olive Oil* PANCAKE

SERVES 6

There is a stunning resort near my house upstate called Wildflower Farms. It is on the site of a beautiful piece of farmland, and it embodies all that you could ever want from an upstate resort: roaring fire pit, outdoor pool, pin drop-quiet spa, and a lovely restaurant. The restaurant at the getaway, Clay, serves a big, airy weekend brunch, and I go as often as my schedule allows. One of the items on the menu, the olive oil pancake, is a staple. Nearly every table orders it as an appetizer. It is more cake than pancake, but it is exquisite: fluffy, flavorful, and citrusy, with a crispy-ish outer edge. The amazing team at Clay provided me with their original gluten-free recipe, which I adapted and scaled down to fit in one giant 10-inch cast-iron skillet. This version of "pancaking" is a much less stressful affair than the traditional stovetop method, and it is every bit as good—if not better.

FOR THE PANCAKE

¾ cup (150 g) granulated sugar

1 cup (125 g) all-purpose flour

¼ cup (30 g) rye flour

1 teaspoon baking soda

1 teaspoon salt

½ cup (120 ml) extra-virgin olive oil

⅔ cup (160 ml) whole milk

2 large eggs, room temperature

3 tablespoons orange liqueur, like Grand Marnier

3 tablespoons fresh orange juice

Zest of one orange

1 tablespoon unsalted butter

Place a 10-inch cast-iron skillet in the oven and preheat the oven to 375°F (190°C).

In a large bowl, whisk together the sugar, both flours, baking soda, and salt.

In a medium bowl, whisk together the olive oil, milk, eggs, orange liqueur, orange juice, and orange zest.

Make a well in the dry ingredients and pour the wet ingredients into the well. Using a spoon or spatula (not a whisk), stir, don't beat, the ingredients together until combined and no flour lumps remain. Set the batter aside for 10 minutes.

recipe continues next page

SURE THING NOTE

The cast iron gives this pancake a toasty bottom and sides. You can absolutely bake this in a regular oven-safe nonstick skillet, but the browning effect will be minimal. I am not trying to talk you out of using a traditional skillet, but if you can, seek out or borrow a cast-iron one.

FOR THE PANCAKE TOPPING

2 ounces (4 tablespoons / 55 g) unsalted butter, room temperature

Maple syrup

Whipped cream (optional, page 38)

Extra orange zest (optional)

Once the oven is fully at temperature, remove the skillet and add the tablespoon of butter. Carefully swirl the butter as it melts so that it coats the bottom and edges of the pan.

Pour the batter into the skillet and bake until the the top of the pancake turns a dark brown and a toothpick inserted into the middle of the pancake comes out clean.

Remove from the oven, wait 2 minutes, and invert onto a serving platter.

Serve with butter and maple syrup. I also like to serve with a side of fresh whipped cream sprinkled with orange zest.

MY WEEKEND
MALTED *Buttermilk* WAFFLES

SERVES 8 TO 10

I have been hanging on to this waffle recipe ever since developing a version of it for the second Baked book. It is the sort of recipe I didn't expect be on heavy rotation for me, but it just kind of stuck around. It has become incredibly useful over the years. These waffles take advantage of one of my favorite ingredients, malted milk powder, which adds a hint of sweet toothsome nuttiness to the ordinary waffle flavor. It is entirely possible the malted flavor will take a back seat to your avalanche of waffle toppings, but if you ever eat your waffles plain (i.e., naked waffles), you will be pleased to have them malted. While this may not be a revolutionary waffle recipe, it is beloved.

- 2 cups (240 g) all-purpose flour
- 1 cup (140 g) malted milk powder
- 3 tablespoons firmly packed light brown sugar
- 1 teaspoon baking soda
- 1½ teaspoons baking powder
- ½ teaspoon salt
- 2 large eggs, at room temperature
- 2½ cups (475 ml) buttermilk
- 3 ounces (6 tablespoons / 85 g) unsalted butter, melted and cooled to room temperature
- Maple syrup, butter, and/or chocolate chips for serving

Preheat the oven to 225°F (110°C) and position a wire rack in the center of your oven. Prepare a waffle iron with cooking spray or vegetable oil per the manufacturer's instructions.

In a large bowl, whisk together the flour, malt powder, brown sugar, baking soda, baking powder, and salt.

In a separate medium bowl, whisk the eggs slightly, add the buttermilk and butter, and whisk again.

Make a well in the center of the dry ingredients and pour the buttermilk mixture into it. Fold the dry ingredients into the wet ever so gently until just combined—there will be some visible lumps.

Make sure your waffle iron is at peak temperature. Depending on the size of your waffle iron, you will most likely need between ¼ to ½ cup of batter per waffle. I use a dry cup measurement to measure and pour the batter into the center of the waffle iron and cook the waffle according to the manufacturer's instructions. The waffles are done when they are golden brown or (my preference) just a little darker.

After you complete each waffle, transfer it to a wire rack in your warm oven in a single layer.

Serve warm with maple syrup, butter, and/or chocolate chips.

SURE THING NOTE

Make sure your waffle iron is extremely hot. A well-done waffle should be, um, well-done. The darker the better, in my opinion. It is important to bring your waffle iron back to its full temperature before adding the next round of batter.

THE *Anything Goes* FRUIT MUFFIN

MAKES 6 JUMBO OR 12 REGULAR MUFFINS

I am slightly horrified to think back to my first years in New York City—fresh out of college—where each and every morning I happily ate an oversized lemon-flavored deli muffin, wrapped in plastic and most likely made before the turn of the century. Was the muffin over 2000 calories? Probably. Was it filled with an ingredient list that owes a great deal to science? Yes, I can most certainly guarantee it.

Since this time, I have dialed my muffin intake down. Now, I only make muffins for weekends or special morning get-togethers. They are still one of my favorite things to make, and I tailor each batch for the moment or the guests. Think of this recipe as your base model. It will produce a delicious, satisfying muffin as is, but maybe you want to add some warm spices during the winter months? Or, perhaps, some lemon zest in the spring? Or, go ahead and swap the mixed berries for a handful of chocolate chips. Make it your own.

- 2 cups (250 g) all-purpose flour
- ½ cup (100 g) granulated sugar, plus more for topping (optional)
- ½ cup (110 g) light brown sugar
- 2 teaspoons baking powder
- ½ teaspoon baking soda
- ½ teaspoon salt
- 4 ounces (8 tablespoons / 115 g) unsalted butter, melted and slightly cool
- 8 ounces (225 g) sour cream
- 2 large eggs
- 1 teaspoon vanilla extract
- 2 cups mixed berries (fresh or frozen), plus more for topping

Preheat the oven to 400°F (200°C) and position a rack in the center. Grease every other well in a 6-cup muffin tin with nonstick cooking spray, making sure it coats the bottom and sides of each well evenly. Do not use muffin liners.

In a medium bowl, whisk together the flour, both sugars, baking powder, baking soda, and salt.

In another bowl, whisk together the melted butter, sour cream, eggs, and vanilla extract until combined.

Toss the mixed berries into the dry mix and fold them in so they are evenly dispersed.

Fold the wet ingredient mixture into the dry ingredients until just blended and a few dry streaks remain.

Divide half the batter evenly among the greased muffin cups. Set aside the other half of the batter. I use a small ice-cream scoop with a release mechanism to make portioning into the cups less messy.

Sprinkle the top of the muffin batter with a few berries and sugar.

Bake in the preheated oven for 5 minutes, then reduce the oven temperature to 350°F (180°C) and bake for another 15 minutes or until a toothpick inserted into the center of a muffin comes out clean or with a few crumbs.

Remove the muffins from the oven, let them cool for 10 minutes in the pan, then release them onto a wire rack dome side up to cool completely. Yes, you can certainly eat these warm.

Fill the pan again with the remaining batter—every other cup—and bake using the same method as the first batch (i.e., increase the oven temperature to 400°F / 200°C before reducing, etc.).

Wrapped tightly, the muffins can be stored for up to 3 days at room temperature.

SURE THING NOTE

Years after leaving my bakery career, I noticed two social media muffin baking tips that I now employ in my own home baking. I was unable to attribute the original tipsters, but their knowledge does not go unnoticed. Both tips promise a bit more height out of your muffins. First, bake the muffins in a 400°F / 200°C oven for a few minutes to amplify the leaveners. You reduce the temperature five minutes into baking. Second, only fill every other muffin cup, so the muffins get more evenly baked and have more room to "grow."

Banana Chocolate Chip MUFFINS: THE SURE̲S̲T̲ THING

SERVES 8

If there was ever a recipe that qualified for The Surest Thing, this would be it. It is effortless, endlessly forgiving, and it is truly crowd-pleasing. I have zero hard data to support this, but I believe this is one of the most frequently made recipes from any of my previous books, and with good reason. Not only is it easy—no equipment needed—but it is also a perfect bite-size banana chocolate treat that somehow feels necessary and guilt-free. The espresso was added to counteract the sweetness and also lend a "morning" element, but you could easily skip this not-always-in-the-pantry ingredient. Lastly, these things freeze like little gems. Pop them into a freezer bag and just pull one out each morning while you make your morning coffee.

- 1½ cups (360 g) mashed very ripe bananas (about 4 medium bananas)
- ½ cup (100 g) granulated sugar
- ¼ cup packed (55 g) light brown sugar
- 4 ounces (8 tablespoons / 115 g) unsalted butter, melted
- ¼ cup (60 ml) whole milk
- 1 large egg
- 1½ cups (195 g) all-purpose flour
- 1 teaspoon instant espresso powder (sometimes I add up to 3 teaspoons, other times I just leave it out)
- 1½ teaspoons baking soda
- 1 teaspoon kosher salt
- 1 cup (170 g) dark or semisweet chocolate chips

Preheat the oven to 350°F (180°C) and position a rack in the center. Spray a 12-cup muffin pan with nonstick baking spray. Do not use muffin liners.

In a medium bowl, stir together the bananas, granulated and brown sugars, butter, milk, and egg.

In another medium bowl, whisk together the flour, instant espresso powder, if using, baking soda, and salt. Make a well in the middle of the dry ingredients. Pour the wet ingredients into the well and stir until just combined. Fold in the chocolate chips. Use a medium ice-cream scoop with a release mechanism to fill each cup about three-quarters full.

Bake for 20 to 25 minutes, until a toothpick inserted in the center of a muffin comes out clean.

Move the muffin pan to a cooling rack and let cool for 15 minutes. After 15 minutes, remove the muffins from the pan and let them finish cooling on the cooling rack, domed side up. Wrapped tightly, the muffins can be stored for up to 2 days at room temperature.

SURE THING NOTE

No notes here. Just make sure your bananas are well and ripe—just this side of black is what you are aiming for.

A REASONABLE COFFEE CAKE *with* COCOA CRUMB

SERVES 12

There are few things more comforting than a slice of coffee cake. It is not a fancy dessert. In fact, it is decidedly old-fashioned without being retro or cool, but it is all you would ever want in an early morning or midafternoon snack. My take on the classic coffee cake is approachable, unfussy, and delectable. Like all good grandma-style coffee cakes, I start with a light sour cream sponge, but I added a bit of cocoa powder to both the cinnamon swirl filling and crunchy crumb topping. This gives the cake a bit of color and contrast and a whiff—just a whiff—of chocolaty undertones. A key factor in all good coffee cakes, the cake to crumb ratio, is optimal here. There is always an urge to push the crumb to obscene heights, but the payoff is only ever visual and adds nothing to the final product.

FOR THE CHOCOLATE CINNAMON SWIRL:

- ¼ cup (50 g) granulated sugar
- ¼ cup packed (55 g) light brown sugar
- 2 tablespoons unsweetened Dutch-process cocoa powder
- 1½ teaspoons ground cinnamon

FOR THE CHOCOLATE CRUMB TOPPING:

- ¾ cup (95 g) all-purpose flour
- ¼ cup (50 g) granulated sugar
- ¼ cup packed (55 g) light brown sugar
- ¾ teaspoon ground cinnamon
- 2 tablespoons unsweetened cocoa powder
- 2 ounces (4 tablespoons / 55 g) unsalted butter, melted

MAKE THE CHOCOLATE CINNAMON SWIRL

In a small bowl, whisk together the granulated and brown sugars, cocoa powder, and cinnamon. Set aside.

MAKE THE CHOCOLATE CRUMB TOPPING

In a medium bowl, whisk together the flour, granulated and brown sugars, cinnamon, and cocoa powder until somewhat uniform. Pour the melted butter over the flour mixture. Use your hands to incorporate the melted butter into the mix by squeezing together fistfuls of the mixture until evenly distributed and clumpy crumbs form. Place the bowl in the refrigerator while you make the cake.

MAKE THE SOUR CREAM CAKE

Preheat the oven to 350°F (180°C) and position a rack in the center. Butter the sides and bottom of one 9-inch (23-cm) cake pan and line the bottom with parchment paper. Butter the paper.

In a medium bowl, whisk together the flour, baking powder, baking soda, and salt. Set aside.

In the bowl of a stand mixer fitted with the paddle attachment, cream the butter until smooth and ribbonlike, about 4 to 6 minutes. Scrape down the bowl and add the granulated sugar. Beat on medium speed until the mixture is smooth and starts to look fluffy. Add the eggs, one at a time, beating well after each addition. Scrape down the bowl and mix again for 30 seconds.

recipe continues next page

FOR THE SOUR CREAM CAKE:

- 1¾ cups (215 g) all-purpose flour
- ½ teaspoon baking powder
- ¾ teaspoon baking soda
- ½ teaspoon kosher salt
- 4 ounces (8 tablespoons / 115 g) unsalted butter, slightly cooler than room temperature (20 minutes out of the refrigerator), cut into 1-inch cubes
- 1¼ cups (250 g) granulated sugar
- 2 large eggs
- 8 ounces (225 g) sour cream
- 1 teaspoon pure vanilla extract

Add the sour cream and vanilla and beat on medium speed just until incorporated. Add the dry ingredients in two additions, scraping down the bowl before each addition and beating only until each addition is just incorporated. Do not overmix.

Scoop out half of the cake batter into the prepared pan. I use a medium ice-cream scoop with a release mechanism to portion out the batter into a few small mounds. Then I use an offset spatula to spread the batter evenly across the pan.

Sprinkle the chocolate cinnamon swirl mixture over the batter, covering the entire surface of the batter. Portion the remaining cake batter over the swirl mixture and spread it evenly (again, I think the ice-cream scoop and offset spatula method works best here). Sprinkle the crumb topping evenly over the top of the batter.

Bake for 35 to 40 minutes, until a toothpick inserted in the center of the cake comes out clean. Let the cake cool in the pan on a wire rack for at least 30 minutes before serving.

The cake will keep tightly covered at room temperature for up to 3 days.

SURE THING NOTES

Two small call-outs here: One, the cake really keeps beautifully and is nearly as perfect on day two as it is on day one, so feel free to make ahead of time. Two, you can easily skip the cocoa powder in both the crumb and swirl if you are cocoa-powder adverse, but I urge you not to.

ALMOND BUTTER *Granola*

MAKES 1 POUND (450 G)

Lately, during the long stretches of summer, I default to a simple lunch of Greek yogurt topped with bananas, a sprinkling of hemp or flax seeds or both, and chunky granola. I work from home, and it is an easy enough lunch to prepare. No oven necessary. However, before the work week starts, I try to whip up a batch of this protein-packed cluster-style granola so my ordinary lunches have a touch of the homemade. A version of this granola, branded under Baked (the small bakery I co-founded), was sold far and wide to both mom and pop retailers and big specialty chains alike. For a million-odd reasons, the wholesale effort was never our focus, and it was perpetually underfunded, so when we cut our losses and stopped selling this granola, I was surprised to hear from so many customers that they missed the granola dearly. Herewith is the recipe. It is so easy, so delicious, and fairly forgiving.

- 2 cups (180 g) old-fashioned rolled oats
- 1 teaspoon ground cinnamon
- 1 teaspoon kosher salt
- ¼ cup (60 ml) extra-virgin olive oil
- ¼ cup (60 ml) almond butter
- ¼ cup (60 ml) honey
- ¼ cup packed (55 g) light brown sugar
- 1 teaspoon pure vanilla extract
- ½ cup (70 g) whole almonds
- 1 tablespoon flax seeds
- 1 tablespoon hemp seeds

Preheat the oven to 325°F (160°C) and position a rack in the center. Line a baking sheet with parchment paper.

In a large bowl, toss the oats with the cinnamon and salt.

In a medium bowl, whisk together the olive oil, almond butter, honey, brown sugar, and vanilla until combined. Pour over the oat mixture and use your hands to combine them: Gather up some of the mixture in each hand and make a fist. Repeat until all of the oats are coated with the almond butter mixture. Ideally you should have a few big chunks among the smaller ones. Pour the mixture onto the prepared baking sheet. Spread it out evenly, but leave a few clumps here and there for texture.

Bake for 10 minutes, then remove from the oven and use a metal spatula to lift and flip the granola. Sprinkle the almonds over the granola and return the baking sheet to the oven. Note: If you are using roasted almonds, you can just sprinkle them over the granola mixture with the flax and hemp seeds.

recipe continues next page

Bake for another 5 minutes, then remove from the oven and use a metal spatula to lift and flip the granola. Bake for 10 final minutes, then remove from the oven.

Let cool completely. Sprinkle the flax seeds and hemp seeds over the granola and transfer to an airtight container.

The granola will keep for at least a week, but I have had it for up to 2 weeks, and it was equally as good.

SURE THING NOTE

These days almond butter comes in a variety of forms. I tend to purchase the one-ingredient (no added sugar, no stabilizers, no extra salt) offerings so I have more flexibility when baking with it. However, almost any variety of almond butter will work with this recipe—it will just be sweeter or saltier if those are added ingredients. Also, I have made this with peanut butter and peanuts—subbing out the almond butter and almonds one for one—and it was lovely.

ACKNOWLEDGMENTS

This is my sixth (YIKES) cookbook and my first one flying solo. While I suppose some authors find the writing and development flows easier with each successive volume, I still find the process daunting. I inevitably eat too much during the testing phase and worry too much during the editing phase. In sum, I gain weight and sleep poorly until the book is complete and slated for publication. Once published, I relax and regulate my eating. But honestly, the anxiety ride is worth it. I thoroughly enjoy (who wouldn't) seeing the book on store shelves, and more importantly seeing folks utilize the recipes within.

It would be impossible to birth this cookbook without the slate of friends, family, and professional acquaintances listed here:

First, a big fat shout out to Alex Roberts. He is a dessert whisperer. He is a pastry magician. He helped me conceive a variety of recipes for this book and each one is a keeper (I fear I may have an addiction to the Chocolate Malted Rye Loaf). Check out Alex's socials (@alexanderbakes) and bake along with him. He is charming, and his baking is all vibes, nothing twee.

Also, I want to shout out Cynthia Jordan, pastry princess, for helping me develop a portion of the recipes in this book that needed Cynthia's love and watchful eye. I have known Cynthia since the Baked (the bakery I co-founded three hundred years ago) days, and she has always been a trusted advisor. Her reimagining of the cornbread blondie will always be part of my dessert trophy case.

I need to send all the hugs to my favorite Scotsman, David Armstrong. He kept me sane and in-check during a very busy writing/testing period which coincided with a very busy personal/business period. I love you, David, and all the lemon drizzle cakes.

Thanks to my super-agent, Alison Fargis at Stonesong. We have been working together since my first book, and we have become close friends and confidantes. Alison never takes her pedal off the gas, and I would probably still be typing into the void without her guidance and gusto.

Nate Stearns is a very close friend and valuable recipe tester, even though he thinks every cake should be overly moist. Nate's invisible extra touches are throughout the book, and it is a better book because of him.

Thank you, Dimity Jones, for your diligent testing and honest feedback during a whirlwind two-week period. You deserve a medal for just making it through so many bakes in such a short period of time. If only I could learn via osmosis your time management and organizational skills.

Extra Special Thanks to the Entire Creative Team

Kudos to Dana Gallagher for the stunning photography. You captured the essence of the book's ethos in brilliant photo after brilliant photo. A friend noted that some of the recipe photos look "lickable," and that is the greatest compliment a cookbook writer could receive.

Thank you, Frances Boswell, for reading my mind. Your food styling nuance and prop suggestions made each recipe stand out. I will be forever grateful for your choice to slather my Posh Chocolate Cake in spreadable ice cream. Big hugs to Cynthia Gasparre for your much needed assist on the craziest shoot schedule.

Finally, a big round of applause to my extremely patient editor, Holly Dolce. She expertly shepherded this book through its various incarnations and provided big doses of enthusiasm when I needed it most. And it goes without saying that Abrams has a small but mighty team pulling this all together into a coherent, readable cookbook. Thank you, Hannah Braden, Jodi Wong, Danielle Youngsmith, Diane Shaw, and Deb Wood.

INDEX

C

D

E

F

G

H

I

J

L

M

N

O

P

Q

R

S

T

U

V

W

Y